THE AVENUE:A PERSONAL

DICTIONARY

BY JEFFREY A. KELLY

THE AVENUE: A PERSONAL

DICTIONARY

AVENUE:

ACTUAL DEFINITION- A BROAD ROAD IN A TOWN OR CITY,TYPICALLY HAVING TREES AT REGULAR INTERVALS ALONG ITS SIDES

A WAY OF APPROACHING A PROBLEM OR MAKING PROGRESS TOWARD SOMETHING

MY DEFINITION - OUTLET TO PEACE

PERSONAL:

ACTUAL DEFINITION - OF, AFFECTING OR BELONGING TO A PARTICULAR PERSON RATHER THAN TO ANYONE ELSE

OF OR CONCERNING ONES PRIVATE LIFE, RELATIONSHIPS,

AND EMOTIONS RATHER THAN MATTERS, CONNECTED WITH

ONES PUBLIC OR PROFESSIONAL CAREER

MY DEFINITION - HARD TO DISCUSS AT TIMES, BUT CAN BE

FREEING WHEN DONE

I chose the title, "The Avenue", because this book details the literal road I walked within towards the path of a healthier relationship with myself and the universe.

When I first came up with the idea for this book, the name was the easiest part to conceptualize. As you will soon learn, the process that led to manifestation of this book was much more difficult for me get a grip on. This book is literally and figuratively my pathway to peace. All my experiences and thoughts that are written further in, are my truth and the furthest thing from fabricated; so I ask that you indulge without judgement. We are all working towards something in life (I hope) and the road we travel is tumultuous as hell, no matter what the end goal is. This book is the clearest reflection of my journey and how I have interpreted the lows as well as the highs that I have experienced. My story is not the most unique (in my opinion), but it is definitely relatable. I do not touch on literally everything I have been through, but by the time you get to the very last page, you will leave this book behind with a clearer understanding of who I am compared to what you have currently expected. Through the way the words are structured in this "dictionary", I feel I have painted a clear enough of picture of who Jeff Kelly is, who I was in the past, and who I ultimately want to become.

I am the embodiment of an individual who is just trying to figure out this thing we call life while dealing with his mental health issues/insecurities. I am desperately trying to understand myself and I want to know concretely why I exist; I have been lost for too long. I need answers, and the only way I can find them is if I look within. I have used external sources such as therapy, relationships, friendships as outlets to attempt to find myself but none of them helped fully. In the past, I figured the best view of who I am would come from an outside source, but no answers were ever found. No matter what I did, I would still be caught up in the confusion. I would still be repeating my bad habits and I could not understand why. I had to force myself into a self-reflective state in order to find the change/answers I desire, and this book was the result. Use me as an example of what not to be (or what to be if I at some point inspire you) and apply any of what you read into your own life in your own way. My main hope is that after reading this book, the honesty I express inspires you to self-reflect and find your own reasoning as to why you are who you are. Indulge without judgment but with the understanding that what you are about to read might be one of the most interesting, engaging, yet worst experiences of your life.

Thank you for dedicating your time to reading this, and I truly hope you enjoy your stay on The Avenue.

ABOUT THE AUTHOR

I am Jeffrey Kelly, a 28-year-old Black American man who did not know himself that well before writing this book. Through multiple therapy sessions, conversations with friends and family about who I am and my behavior, as well as writing this book, the answer to who I am has become a bit clearer. I was speeding down the path of self-destruction with the fear of never knowing who I was or why I set myself on this path to begin with scared me the most. The journey to learn, understand, and accept oneself is a never-ending experience, but I had to walk this road. Prolonging the walk in the darkness would have internally and externally killed me. This book was a step in the right direction for me, but even at the end of the experience of cultivating my first book, I still have so much to work on.

In the books I have read in my lifetime, this section of the book is typically written in third person and filled with Snapple facts, stats, and achievements about the author - but not in this book. All you need to know about me is what's written in this book. What I have done previously in my life and what state I was born in is irrelevant and does not compare to what I plan to share in this book as well as every other book I plan to release going forward. As you continue to read this book, who I am will be revealed to you rather quickly, and by the end of this book, you will be left with a choice to accept or reject the author you learned about. So rather than me trying to cram my life story into this one section, turn to the next page, read without judgment, and really learn about the author. Enjoy your stay in my mind.

CHAPTER 1-QUITTING

1-QUITTING

ACTUAL DEFINITION - EXISTING IN FACT; TYPICALLY, AS CONTRASTED WITH WHAT WAS INTENDED; EXPECTED OR BELIEVED.

MY DEFINITION - A THOUGHT THAT HAS CROSSED MY MIND AND HEART MANY TIMES BUT IT IS SOMETHING THAT IS NOT AN OPTION...EVER.

I almost quit again. This book almost never existed. This book, *The Avenue: A -Personal Dictionary,* almost never saw the light of day, and it would have been all my fault. The details of why this book almost never existed will be sprinkled in the next chapter, but what I will say is, act when your mind first conjures the motivation to do something or you'll regret it for the rest of your life. When you first get that sliver of motivation to do anything, whether it's as small as cleaning your room or walking the dog, do it immediately. Do NOT allow yourself to get lazy and waste time.

So now I will pose a question to you. Take as long as you need to formulate an answer before you decide to continue to read. Take a deep breath and ask yourself. *Why do we quit?* I am sure the answer varies from each vessel to the next, but for me personally, I quit because it is hard to convince my mind there are any alternate versions to the ending that has occurred and the fear of even trying to change the outcome takes over me and I do nothing but wallow in despair.

When you pour so much energy into a task (like this book that has been a four-year long process) it's hard to distribute anything you have left to anything else you might have a passion for. To act strong, to dust yourself off and try again is a very difficult concept for my mind to accept. When you work so hard and it is all for naught, it becomes difficult to conjure- then maintain- the confidence that you need to replicate or exceed the work you previously put in. Then, that lingering, fearful feeling of failure is the reason I believe people halt themselves from achieving true comfort within themselves and the universe.

This is my second time writing the first chapter of this book and in all honesty, there's not much confidence in these words (as you continue to read, I get my mojo back) and I have so much fear that another random occurrence will happen that will cause all of this to disappear again. Repeated unplanned and unexpected situations breed the most fear within. I get more comfortable with the idea of quitting as the breeding feeling in the back of my head causes me to overthink my next five moves. The fear of not knowing what's next for me after my first failed attempt causes me to remain stagnant in my pursuit to try again.

The idea of quitting is bred from fear; but what if something different happens after things do not go your way and you are left with a clearer head than the one you began with? This is exactly what happened to me. I lost all the work I put into the original copy of this book that I started two years prior to writing this, and at first, I was left with anger...pure rage and disappointment. So much rage in fact that I ended up screaming at the top of my lungs in a best buy parking lot. Not my finest moment, but losing my work felt equivalent to losing a life to me. At some point, however, the rage subsided (way quicker than I am used to) and suddenly I felt a sense of peace and relief on the inside. Don't they say its calmest and quietest in the middle of a tornado or something like that? That is exactly what it felt like inside of my head post rage. What started out as the most frustrating experience of my life morphed into motivation to start over and do what I could while I had the opportunity to do so.

The first version of this book was equally as personal, but it got to a certain point where I only kept working on it because I wanted it done. I wanted to prove to myself that if I committed to something, I could do it. The frustration was bred from a feeling that I had let myself down, but I kept going and the first result of that will move forward is this first chapter. This chapter is not meant to come off as or be compared to an advice column on how to not quit things, but what I will say is just because things don't go your way in a moment of time, doesn't mean you should forget that you have many more moments ahead that outweigh that one moment that didn't go your way. Find the quiet pocket inside your tornado of sadness and frustration and transmute that energy into something more beneficial and powerful than the energy you initially put in. Life is long as fuck if you want it to be, so do not get stuck and definitely don't quit. I had to traverse all the negative emotions I kept inside after "failing" in order to come to the realization that quitting is not an option, ever. I will fail again. I may even lose all my work again, but my life will still be intact which means there's room for more opportunities to make stuff happen for me. Perseverance, understanding, and the lack of belief in the idea of quitting is needed in order to ascend. These encouraging words are coming from a consistent quitter, so if I can learn and adapt to these beliefs, you definitely can. I convinced my mind quitting was a safer option to avoid further disappointment, but I was wrong. Quitting was more painful than the potential failure I thought was heading my way. If only

I kept going through those moments prior to quitting, I am sure I would have surprised myself. Quitting provides zero form of comfort; fight through the idea that quitting is an option and keep going. That last sentence is something I would tell my younger self repeatedly, if I had the chance.

CHAPTER 2-PROCASTINATION

02-PROCRASTINATION

ACTUAL DEFINITION - THE ACTION OF DELAYING OR POSTPONING SOMETHING.

MY DEFINITION - A BAD IDEA. DON'T DO THIS IF YOU CAN.

I am a resident, mayor, and president of procrastination nation. The worst joke ever but it is beyond true. Let me give you two examples of my procrastination and how it screwed me over in the end. I promise I will make this as brief as possible, and at the end of these examples (if you aren't already), I hope that you will do your best to own your individualism and NOT follow in my footsteps. Do NOT keep the cycle of procrastination going. Let us start with the inception of this book and how long it took me to actually sit down and start.

This book started off as three other ideas prior to the concept that it is right now, with the first idea manifested back in the year 2015. During that time, I was not doing much with my life besides working two jobs and attending school part time online. I did not go out much, so I had no excuse not to start with the concept I had. The excuse that I always gave myself was "I had a long day, I will put it off to tomorrow" …and that continued all the way to the end of 2015. Transitioning into 2016, nothing was done at all, thus that was the end of the first concept of this book.

The second concept before this one was manifested early 2016. It was solidified and outlined pretty early on in the year, and all I had to do was go and get a new laptop. That is it. Sounds SUPER easy right? I mean someone who was decent at saving their money and had two decent paying jobs around that time should have had no problem just going to a store (a store where he got 15% off) and buying a new computer. I should've had zero issues just going. Right? Well technically, but when you are an immense over-thinker *and* do not get off your ass, the combination is paralyzing. For no reason other than allowing myself to be consumed by the "what ifs" and "I'm lazy", nothing came from it for another year.

That brings us to the concept you have in your hand today. This idea was conceptualized in 2017 (shocker) but it took a lot to actually sit down and begin - not for any excuse other than again (drum roll please) laziness and overthinking.

Here is a bonus example for procrastination that ties in with *Chapter 1- Quitting.* After actually starting this book, I was 30 chapters deep and the laptop I was using before this one ended up getting a cracked screen and dying (don't get drunk/high around your electronics). I ended up having to take it to a local Best Buy to get all the data transferred from the dead laptop to a USB that I could THEN move over to the new one I acquired, and I could finally finish this book. Guess what happened? I got it transferred to the USB but didn't immediately get back to work for whatever reason and I ended up losing the USB with all the data. Thus detouring the progression of this book and causing me to start over and manifest what you have today.

All I had to do was act and not think. If you have learned anything from any of this, it should be do not procrastinate or you will regret it and end up screaming at the top of your lungs in your car in a Best Buy parking lot like I did. I hope you also learned that procrastination is a curse not easily shaken until results are shown, because once I started, I didn't stop and now you have what I put off for damn near four years. What an exhausting and self-destructive four years it has been. Sorry for the wait. *shrugs*

CHAPTER 3-ABANDONMENT

03-ABANDONMENT

ACTUAL DEFINITION – THE ACTION OR FACT OF ABANDONING OR BEING ABANDONED

MY DEFINITION – ONE OF THE MOST HEART WRENCHING, GUT PUNCHING, HORRIBLE FEELINGS SOMEONE CAN EXPERIENCE, ESPECIALLY A CHILD.

28 years ago, the man who played a part in creating me abandoned my mother and I while she was pregnant with me. With no warning or hesitation, he left without a word and till this very day, while I write this, we literally have no idea why he left or where he is located. As I've gotten older and have seen this same scenario in films and have heard stories of young couples with a whole lot of ambition and not enough money to properly provide, I can sit back and really understand why the thought of being selfish is way more appealing than putting your goals on hold to support a woman (you may not or may not really be into) and a child that wasn't on your radar at all. Maybe it is because I am an overly ambitious individual, but the

thought of not having the time, funds, or energy to pursue my goals is truly one of the scariest thoughts my mind could ever conjure. However, I am also self-aware enough to know the concept of consequence is always present in any decision we make.

On the flip side of the coin of life choices, I cannot understand a man - who decided to indulge in this woman's life and ultimately create a life with this woman, whether it was planned or not, could not think far ahead enough and question how this child's mental state would be without him around. How could you not think the wisdom and information you hold could extend and expand upon the child's life and change the trajectory of their future? How could you not think the selfish side of your mind would not be a perfect lesson to show your child how they should not think/be? How could you not think you being around, even if it were once a week, would not be the most important thing to that child regardless if you and his mother didn't have a perfect relationship?

These are all questions I had when I was old enough to realize I was not like every other kid in my neighborhood. When I looked around and truly noticed that I did not come from a two-parent home like my peers, it made me extremely sad. It made me so sad in fact, I actually stopped associating myself with kids who were my friends who had two parent homes. It made me so jealous and sad I could not stand to see it. When I was old/confident enough to attempt to sort through this flurry of negative thoughts that clouded my mind for years, only then was I ready to start the healing process. The one thought that consistently appeared in my mind was the thought that I was the reason for their split. Till this day, I do not know the connection they had. I do not know how serious it was and what plans they had for each other, but I always felt like my existence was the reason why their relationship was strained enough for him to leave without a word. I always felt guilty for being alive and believed my existence would bring more negativity than positivity to people's lives. The relationship with my mother for the majority of my life has always been a bit awkward especially growing up. She worked a lot in order to afford to care of me which naturally meant she wasn't "around" as much I wanted. So my mind created this narrative of the relationship I wanted with my mother mixed with the harsh reality of the negative connection we had for a large chunk of my life. We did not have many moments where we interacted or had many times to really get to know one another. I felt as if she was a stranger at times, and my desire to get to know someone I did not feel I knew was nonexistent and a bit scary. I internalized this reality I created as a kid as confirmation that I was the reason for their split and deep down, I always felt she resented me. I had no proof other than the evidence my mind manifested for me.

As you can see, when you're an only child, you have a lot of conversations in your head and you create realities that can be completely eliminated just by having a conversation and asking questions - something I was too scared to attempt. All these dark thoughts were birthed from not having a father around in my life. Subconsciously, I suppressed the real hurt and sadness I felt about this situation, but through therapy and brief conversations I eventually had with my mother, I have grown comfortable with my existence. Truthfully, not having a father around was the biggest blessing in disguise I could ever ask for. I was given the blueprint of who I should not be and how I will not act when I ultimately have my own children. It is a bit ironic that my purpose with this book is partly to be an example of what not to think/not to be. To those who experience something similar, just know you are NOT alone, and it is NOT your fault. The way the cards were laid out for your existence were not in your control, so do not waste your time blaming an external force or yourself internally. Embrace the life you were given and use what you lacked as an example of what you want your children's lives to be.

CHAPTER 4-ACCOUNTABILITY

ACTUAL DEFINITION - THE FACT OR CONDITION OF BEING ACCOUNTABLE

MY DEFINITION - NEEDED TO MAINTAIN STABLE RELATIONSHIPS

Holding yourself accountable for the things that go wrong in your life is a really hard pill to swallow, and although a few particulars may have been involved, I hold myself completely accountable for every failed relationship I have ever had in my life. I have had the honor of involving myself with some of the most incredible women I will probably ever encounter in this lifetime and I played a major role in the separation of these relationships. Knowing who you are and having an idea of who you think you are, are two different things. I feel throughout my life, I met women who knew who they were completely while I was still in the learning phase of my existence. Not knowing myself had me acting certain ways during these relationships that I was not even aware I was doing until it was pointed out by my partner - which would in turn cause me to react against their feelings in a combative manner. I fought against the truth and lost every solid relationship I had. My inability to communicate was also a toxic habit that caused my relationships to crumble. I did not know how to communicate when something was wrong, I just dealt with it. I was used to being a walking mat for others, so I just let what bothered me stay inside. I would half ass my honesty and not fully share my true feelings which would cause my true feelings to fester and eventually explode into one argument that had no relevance to the feelings I held within. This would lead to a more intense drawn-out argument that typically ended with me being wrong and apologetic. These situations are something that I truly take full blame for now but could not accept that this was the truth at the time. I always felt I gave what I required communication wise, but the main moments that caused my partners to comment on my communication skills were when I got stressed. A few of them would always say to me that I don't express when something is wrong, and I just isolate myself in the partnership. Looking back they were right - but I did that for a reason (that I am not trying to justify). I did that because I was always cognizant of the fact that they also had things going on in life and I never wanted to add to that weight of my stress to their load and be a bother. I was continuously told it wasn't fair for me to make that decision. I also have this issue of relating to anyone fully. I always feel like my experiences are mine and mine alone and nobody else can fully understand so I keep my thoughts on the inside as deeply down in my spirit as I can. I refer to myself as terminally unique. I had to learn that a partnership sticks together closely through it all, no matter the circumstance. If both people are committed, it can be worked out; I never felt worthy of that commitment. So out of fear, I kept it all on the inside out of fear losing my partner. I did not realize until it was too late that I was so wrong for this way of thinking considering there were women in my life who genuinely gave a fuck about me. Who while they may not have fully understood me if I explained my feelings, they were willing to try for the sake of the relationship. I let my past scars invade my relationships and while I thought I was the best boyfriend in the world, in reality, I was the most toxic individual in the universe.

My behavior was so beyond what self-aware was that those relationships probably ended way sooner than they could have because of it. Self-analyze before sharing energy and time with someone else because if you do not come correct, you'll do nothing but be selfish and potentially leave someone with more emotional scars than he or she came into the situation with. Hold yourself accountable for the things that go wrong in your life. Of course sometimes things are out of our control but always ask the question, "What role did I play to get us here?" To all my exes who I was not my best self for, I truly apologize, and I hold myself accountable for the end of those relationships. I argued against the truth too many times, but on the other end of those relationships, my exes have an example

of the type of person they do not want to be with. I left those situations

as an example of who I do not want to be, and I couldn't have come to

this realization without any one of those relationships. A mutually,

painful learning lesson. Face the truth and hold yourself accountable

no matter how large or small the situation is or remain unhappy and

lonely.

5-ATTITUDE

05-ATTITUDE

ACTUAL DEFINITION - A SETTLED WAY OF THINKING OR FEELING ABOUT SOMEONE OR SOMETHING, TYPICALLY ONE THAT IS REFLECTED IN A PERSON'S BEHAVIOR

MY DEFINITION - MANIFESTS FROM PEOPLES STUPID BEHAVIOR. I HAVE ONE. DON'T ANNOY ME

I have an extremely bad and disgusting attitude at times. One of the triggers that causes my attitude to conjure is when people are disrespectful to me or anyone that I love. I will never tolerate disrespect from anyone I know personally or do not know at all. If you have the confidence to go out of your way to treat me or my people with disrespect, it means you know exactly what you're doing and aren't fearful of the consequences. Those consequences include me returning the favor and giving them a healthy heaping of disrespect. I am self-aware enough to know that my perception of peoples' words/intentions are misconstrued at times and I have given people an attitude and taken things as disrespect when in reality they weren't, and it has caused unnecessary conflict but hey…nobody's perfect.

COME CORRECT OR NOT AT ALL.

Another prime example of something that gives me an attitude is when someone does not cover their mouth when they cough, sneeze, or yawn; you can also throw in when people don't chew with their mouth closed. ALL OF THIS DRIVES ME CRAZY WHEN I'M SURROUNDED BY SOMEONE WHO DOES SHIT LIKE THIS. Not only are you putting me at risk by spreading your germs, but you are also putting others at risk as well and it is just outright selfish of you to think that is okay! If you're reading this and are consistently not covering your mouth when you cough, sneeze, yawn, or when you are chewing your food, I want you to know that I personally hate you without knowing anything about you. That is a disrespectful and disgusting act and I have an attitude just thinking about it. Lastly, the one thing that I will say for sure gives me an attitude is when people LIE. I'm not perfect and I have definitely lied before and gotten caught in one, so maybe I am not allowed to get mad at something I am guilty of, but it still doesn't make it hurt any less or less annoying. People lie out desperation and fear and usually do it to avoid any consequences. 10 times out of 10, karma catches up to them and the truth is revealed. I've learned people lie without even knowing that they are. It's second nature to them and their perception of reality is completely warped and those type of individuals aren't worth keeping around. They will only hinder your progress in life. I am sure someone I have lied to is reading this with a confused look. Yes I am being hypocritical while still being honest.

I could continue to go on and on about what gives me an attitude, but this chapter was more of a reflective/therapeutic piece for me. I feel my attitude is stemmed from my judgement of others and that is a terrible trait to have, and I actively want to try to avoid being what I hate. In addition, having an attitude all the time about things causes other people's perceptions of my character to be warped, and although I will not be liked by everyone and their idea of me won't matter in the end, I truly don't ever want to be labeled as the judgmental guy with the attitude all the time. At my core, that is only a sliver of who I am. I need to practice controlling my attitude and let people live and just do my best to avoid anyone who does things that do not align with or benefit my existence. My attitude probably won't ever go away, and neither will the people who do the things that conjure my attitude; so I guess all I can do is have my attitude in private and accept people for who they are. BUT, if you are going to continue to cough without covering your mouth in public, just know I will do my best to avoid you at all costs because that is just fucking disgusting.

Be mindful, be aware, be selfish with your time and conscious of where you distribute your energy and know that having an attitude is

not always warranted but aggressively expressing yourself to

someone who is doing something you don't like may be the key to

helping them be more aware of themselves.

06-AUTHOR

ACTUAL DEFINITION- A WRITER OF A BOOK, ARTICLE, OR
REPORT.

MY DEFINITION-ME....?

If you made it to this chapter in the book for starters, I want to say
THANK YOU. Thank you for being receptive and supportive of my first
tangible idea thus far. This book is literally my thoughts and
experiences in paper/e-book form and you-reading this shows me that
not only is my work accepted, but I am as well. Honestly, I am sure
you never have been thanked by the author six chapters in, but at this
point, I have managed to capture and keep your attention and you
have accepted me a bit.

I think acceptance is what I always yearned for my entire life.
Whether it's from the parent I did have, the parent I did not have, the
girls in school, the popular kids, corporations, or the world, I just
wanted to be accepted. Most importantly, I wanted to accept myself.
To not be judged, hated on, or given the side eye ever in life. All I
want from (almost) everyone I encounter, is for them to accept me at

face value and enjoy the highs and lows of my being. I feel if it hasn't been apparent up till now, I will express how my book has been written thus far is proof that I am not a professional. So before you close this book and puts it on the shelf to let it collect dust till the next book comes out, know that every chapter is 100% my thoughts exactly without any editing or filtering and I really don't know how to say anything other than what's on my mind. If we are abiding by the actual definition of the word author, then being that you made it this far in the book and the fact that it actually exists means there's no way anyone can say anything different, right? I am...an author?! I am not sure how many of you reading this have accomplished something that you have wanted for yourself your entire life, but it is a really trippy experience. A bit scary as well. Putting every bit of your energy and time into something and then getting it, in my experiences provides the question "what is next?" I obviously have way more goals and even more books I want to write but I feel a bit confused as where to go to next. On the flip side of my mind, I feel I haven't even savored this moment, so how can I move on to the next one? I recommend that to all the entrepreneurs/creatives, smell the rose and take a fucking break or something. Pressure sucks!

This book is the first thing I ever committed to and did not give up on no matter how many (MANY) roadblocks that tried to stop this from existing, but it is here and yours for as long as you want it to be. This book can be used as a gift for a loved one if you don't feel like spending money, or a coaster for your coffee. OR (I hope it's this one) as a tool you can refer back to for some form of inspiration, motivation, and peace of mind. Now that this exhausting process is complete, I can finally be free of the immense pressure I put on myself for years on end. THANK GOD AND THANK YOU FOR ACCEPTING ME AND MY ART SO FAR.

07-AWARENESS

07-AWARENESS

ACTUAL DEFINITION - KNOWLEDGE OR PERCEPTION OF A SITUATION OR FACT

CONCERN ABOUT AND WELL-INFORMED INTEREST IN A PARTICULAR SITUATION OR DEVELOPMENT

MY DEFINITION - A NECESSARY COMPONENT FOR GROWTH INTO THE ULTIMATE VERSION OF OURSELVES

Throughout the progression of my life, the one thing I learned very early on is that in order for me to truly ascend to the level I want to be on, all I have to do is remain self-aware at all times. For the longest portion of my life and even today at some points, I move with lack of awareness of self and it affects my mental state and the relationships that I have in my life, mostly in a negative way. What has worked for me to improve my awareness of self may not work for you, but it usually has taken someone outside of myself to point out my behavior and then that allows me to internalize exactly what I'm doing and improve upon that behavior afterwards. I try my best to not let it get to the point where I am getting yelled at and only relying on others to point out my negative traits to grow, but it's helped me a bit.

Secondly, I try to isolate myself and force myself into a state of analysis when things get too bad or I am having multiple people (who don't even know each other most times) saying the same things about my behavior. My overthinking nature, as you could guess, would flare up intensely when multiple comments about how I act is affecting people. So out of fear of losing them and further hurting anyone, I do all I can internally to fix who I am. In this isolation period, most time is spent beating myself up for my behavior, but the rest of time is spent reflecting heavily and forcing myself into a state of acknowledgment of my actions.

The goals I have for myself will require me to connect with new people and build new relationships as well as improve on the ones I currently have; so self-awareness will become harder to align with the more outlets to different opinions I open but it will be even more necessary. Being that a major part of my journey will require me to interact with and build many relationships with people who come from different beliefs, backgrounds, and personalities that I will have to adjust to as time progresses, it wouldn't be fair to them for me to move with no awareness of myself and what I can contribute to the relationship. More so in the past, but still currently at times, I have been a very reactionary type of person. I react to certain things people say based off a negative experience I had with someone else. I have been aware enough to fully realize this and apply what I learned to make the change in my life, so I will not react in a combative way, but it takes time, a lot of it. This is just an example of how self-aware I am that I know I do this, and I also know I don't make an active effort to change and still react to things that are over and done with.

Walking aimlessly through life without fully knowing who you are is one of the most detrimental things you could do to yourself and to the people in your life. Take as much time as you can spending it getting to know who you are and to avoid being like me. I have projected so much of my lack of awareness and insecurities that I hold onto to so many people who genuinely wanted the best for me, and in turn I have hurt (if you happen to be one of them and are reading this, I'm sorry) and I have full regret for those actions, but I also wear them as a badge of experience that I will wear and utilize in order to become the best version of myself. I move through life with a load of guilt that I bear from the amount of pain I caused others that could have been avoided entirely if I knew about myself a bit more, but I know if I try to get to know myself better, I know I will do better going forward in life. Get to know yourself a bit - what you will learn may surprise you.

08-AWKWARD

8-AWKWARD

ACTUAL DEFINITION – CAUSING DIFFICULTY, HARD TO DO OR DEAL WITH

MY DEFINITION - IT CAN'T BE HELPED, SECOND NATURE, ME.

I can be very awkward at times. I legitimately cannot help it and I do not think this part of my personality will ever change. Luckily, I accepted this fact about me years ago. My awkwardness includes saying jokes at the wrong time, being the quietest one in the room full of people who are interacting, fumbling my words, and butchering whatever sentence I attempt to formulate. The most common awkward thing I do is not make eye contact all the time. My awkwardness paired with my overthinking nature makes for an awkward ass life I live. I am self-aware of all these things about myself and I have ended up improving on that awkward behavior and have gotten way better with all those things. I make eye contact way more, but what I have noticed with other people I interact with is that the interactions with people who also make direct eye contact aren't as frequent, so my attempt ends up failing and causes me to overthink and awkwardly look at the ground while attempting to have a full conversation. I still tend to be the quietest one the room, but it is simply for my own comfort these days. I like to interact when I am comfortable and comfortable only. If I attempt to force my extroverted side out when I am not, it will most likely be the worst conversation myself and the other person involved will ever experience. As I am adjusting into a comfortable state within myself, I feel my conversational skills have actually improved when I have chosen to speak only when comfortable. So, what do I do in the chances where I may not have the time to adjust to being comfortable? It is a bit hard to articulate, but it is like an invisible light switch that ticks in my head and I am able to adjust to the conversation by force in order to avoid further awkwardness and discomfort within myself. So, when the switch is flipped, I am able to adjust and force a personable version of myself out but when it's not, I will probably stare and nod awkwardly. This is a hit or miss type of occurrence, most of the time the awkwardness is present the whole time. Lastly, the way I have adjusted/improved upon the messing up of words mid-sentence and completely butchering whatever point I am trying to make is very simple. I have not.

I truly do not think this part of my awkward nature will ever go away. My mind moves way faster than my delivery of words, so I end up saying a thought in the middle of a thought I'm trying to express. Then in turn, those thoughts combine and come out to be a sentence that literally makes no sense at all. This happens to me probably once a week and I have come up with zero ways to fix this problem within me. Slowing down my thinking and taking some time to think before I speak would work but my passion and enthusiasm for a good conversation mixed with a comfortable mood make it hard to resist not just letting my thoughts out without thinking fully. The moral of this story is to embrace your awkward nature with your arms open wide. You can do what you can to adjust to that side of you, and since I haven't seen any ways of getting rid of the awkwardness completely, I figure you should just accept it and move with it side-by-side rather than against it. Embrace the awkwardness.

09-BALANCE

9-BALANCE

ACTUAL DEFINITION - AN EVEN DISTRIBUTION OF WEIGHT ENABLING SOMEONE OR SOMETHING TO REMAIN UPRIGHT AND STEADY

A CONDITION IN WHICH DIFFERENT ELEMENTS ARE EQUAL OR IN THE CORRECT PROPORTIONS

MY DEFINITION- WHAT I AM STRIVING FOR IN EVERY ASPECT OF MY LIFE

Part of my being, my Libra nature forces me to strive towards finding balance in every aspect of my life, but the way life is set up with so many random factors that can shift our whole reality in an instant, in my mind this fact causes the idea of obtaining that balance to be non-existent. I crave a balanced life, but I have a hard time even putting into words what exactly that would like look. Having everything I want out of this life at my fingertips paired with the chances of everything going away in an instant sounds about right, but my mind subconsciously leans toward only having a life where everything goes my way without any chances for disaster. But you and I both know that isn't possible. Some would say balance in one's life starts within. They would say that no matter what type of life I aim to keep balanced, if every aspect of my being is not aligned then, there is no hope for achieving what I am seeking. My response to something like that would agree, but how does one find balance within themself? Someone like me who is trapped in the never-ending maze of my mind; someone like me who is learning about himself at a snail's pace - how the hell do I achieve balance within? What I have learned about myself is that I need to be more comfortable with the "negative" aspects of my existence and I need to take things at face value. I tend to overthink the little things that happen to me and my mind in turn blows these things up into something way bigger than it is equaling to the further demise of my chances at gaining balance. Awareness, acceptance, and appreciation seem to be the key ingredients towards gaining the balance I seek, and I am sure if I continue this snail's pace towards that goal, I will reach it eventually. If you have learned anything from me in this chapter, I hope it is that a balanced life is not bred from an unbalanced individual. Look within and your perception from outside your mind will make your view of your existence way brighter and more balanced than it might seem to be initially. If only I could apply my own wisdom to my own life. The scales of balance will align for me one day as long as I keep trying, right?

10-BLACK

10-BLACK

ACTUAL DEFINITION - OF THE VERY DARKEST COLOR OWING TO THE ABSENCE OF OR COMPLETE ABSORPTION OF LIGHT; THE OPPOSITE OF WHITE

OF ANY HUMAN GROUP HAVING DARK COLORED SKIN, ESPECIALLY OF AFRICAN OR AUSTRRAILIAN ABORIGINAL

MY DEFINITION - BEAUTIFUL

I LOVE BEING BLACK. I LOVE WEARING THIS BLACK SKIN. I was not always able to say that and mean it if I am being honest. Looking up the history of your people and what we have endured - as a youth in my case – embedded in me a fear of being black. As a people, for generations, we have had a target on our back and have been disrespected as well as; it hurt so much it made me feel like the same fate would fall upon my family, and myself eventually. At times it felt like the only way out of that fate was to be someone with lighter skin (white). As I got older, I am so glad I eliminated this way of thinking, and what really made me come to this realization was what got me there in the first place. More and more examples of my people getting killed for no reason other than existing made my empathy deepen, my relatability to be being black increase, and ultimately my fear morphed into a need to protect as well as take pride in who I am and own my blackness. The fear turned into a strength/comfort; the thought that a certain group of people literally hate me and want to eliminate me for my skin color is a crazy thought, but it empowered me. This realization made me want to own my uniqueness even more, being black felt like an honor. To be hated for no reason made me feel special. I don't recall if there was a particular injustice that was the trigger, but when you see situations like with the unfortunate passing of TRAYVON MARTIN or ERIC GARNER or SANDRA BLAND or KALIEF BROWDER or ATATIANA JEFFERSON, it just becomes too much for your soul to bare and it makes you want to fight back against the hate. The hate that exists for black people is not reciprocated, so the need to be on defense at all times was a thought that was easily adjusted, its second nature now. I don't feel safe anywhere I go, I remain on guard no matter where I go.

I've experienced racism through very slight personal experiences; nothing worth sharing but mostly my experiences come through osmosis from the stories I've heard growing up from my grandmother, and everything that was embedded into my mind through research mixed with every time I look up at the television. It is truly frustrating to me that just simply existing causes someone who does not look like me and who does not even know me to hate me and even want to kill me. Baffling. Ignorant. STUPID. Through the hate for my people, my love for myself and my skin grew. It makes me feel invincible amongst all the fear I have. For them to hate me for being me and having this glorious skin...they must be jealous, they must wish they had this. They must wish the influence my culture brings to the planet had their stamp on it.

These thoughts filled my mind and boosted my ego and shaped it into confidence in who I am and increased the appreciation that I had for my existence. This mentality I gained isn't easy to find and maintain especially in the current climate in America. The hate is prevalent and will not go away until the source of it acknowledges the issue and tries to change it from within. I encourage anyone of any age who is BLACK, who feels like I felt, to fight through the negativity and embrace your culture. Own your skin. Love your skin. It is a privilege and honor to be this way and you should wear it like a badge of honor. There is no world without us. There is no culture without us. Black is beautiful. To the non-black folk who are reading this chapter and have not closed the book, know I am not anti you - I am just all for me and my own. I take pride in who I am and where I come from, like I am sure you do. I am not against you, but the source of racism and hate has come from your ancestors and it is your responsibility to go to the source and help end this hate. We just want to live and be

happy like you do. Regardless if racism ends or not, we will exist, and

we still excel. Being black is fucking dope and I am honored to have

this black skin.

11-BLATHERSKITE

11-BLATHERSKITE

ACTUAL DEFINITION - A PERSON WHO TALKS AT GREAT LENGTH WITHOUT MUCH SENSE

MY DEFINITION - A PERSON WHO SHOULD BE AVOIDED AT ALL COSTS

We have all encountered a person like this, but I guarantee 9/10 individuals who are reading this have never heard this word before and I'm NOT trying to discredit your intelligence but who the hell would use any other word to describe this type of individual other than idiot! Being an introverted individual, I tend to listen more times than I choose to talk and for whatever reason. Throughout my life, I've been the approachable type in people's minds, and I have always found myself being talked to for sometimes hours on end by complete strangers. Draining, enlightening, and sometimes a complete waste of time.

I have heard everything from someone complaining about how a restaurant put too much cheese on their CHEESEBURGER to the latest gossip about the Kardashians. The worst/best thing about me is I am super polite and in the past, up till a certain point, I would hear people out and let them get their shit off their chest until I have my opportunity to exit the conversation politely. But as I have gotten older, I've become a lot less tolerant of conversations that don't fuel me at all. The broader topic of this chapter is not to vent about all the terrible conversations I have had throughout my life, but I think the isolated topic that needs to be expressed is adapting the concept of valuing your time/energy and knowing who to share your space with. Most people I connect with I would like to think are similar to me in a sense that they won't be rude, and they'll give someone their time and try to exit a conversation gracefully. I do think that is still the correct way to do things, but I also am all for demanding your peace and being forceful with your exits. I would spend my energy carelessly investing into people and energy that add no benefit to my life. Most times it would be to be polite and others times, especially if the person was close to me, I would indulge in order to not lose them. I value my relationships so deeply I have indulged in energy for years on end that was not a positive influence on my life, and it never became one, but I kept them around.

I feel if you continuously give your time to these pointless conversations, you will adopt that pointlessness subconsciously and start to think you actually care about these things when in reality they are just a distraction. In addition, if you're having these conversations with the same people over and over without telling them how you truly feel, you're giving them permission to do this. If you really value your time/energy, you'll be honest with them and tell them to cut it out. If they appreciate you and value your time as much as they are acting like they do when they invade your space, then they should respect your honesty and move accordingly. We all know a Blatherskite, and I know for a fact we all did not know this word until this chapter. On the flip side of everything I have just said, I am sure people have looked at me as a Blatherskite. Being as emotional and sensitive as I can be, I have vented to many people who I am sure lost track of what I am trying to share or looked at my perception of my problems as insignificant and boring to listen to. While my emotions run high regularly, I am self-aware enough to know I do not make much sense to anyone but myself when I am venting and on that emotional high. I have improved on this in present day but in the past, I never thought about the person I was venting to. Venting is a very selfish act if done unwarranted; you never know what someone else is going through and depending on the type of energy you are spewing their way it may affect them in a negative way. Ask permission before you vent. Reacting emotionally breeds a thought process that makes sense to me and when I am spewing my feelings to someone, they hear my plight but still never truly understand. So in that regard, I am a Blatherskite and have been on many occasions but at least the conversation I am creating is of importance; be careful how you distribute your energy. Be wary of the energy you allow in. Avoid the pointless dialogue at all costs. Meechy Darko from the rap group, Flatbush Zombies, used to do a segment on his Instagram called word of the day and I happened to tune in one day and this was the word he did for a day; it stuck in mind since then and this chapter was the result of that moment. Thanks, Darko and no thanks to the idiotic/pointless conversations we all choose to indulge in/start.

12-CHANGE

12-CHANGE

ACTUAL DEFINITION - MAKE OR BECOME DIFFERENT

TAKE OR USE ANOTHER INSTEAD OF

MY DEFINITION - ON THE WAY, IT WILL COME, IT WILL HAPPEN

SO ADAPT AND ACCEPT

Change is inevitable. No matter how hard we try to resist the currents of time, they keep flowing and we cannot do anything about it. Friends come and go. Opportunities come and go. Relationships come and go. Things do not last forever, and all we are forced to do is keep our heads held high, adapt, and accept the changes no matter how good they are or how painful they are. Sounds fair right? Not at all in my mind. For different reasons, I have had long lasting friendships crumble that I genuinely wanted to last forever. I have lost opportunities that were once in a lifetime chances for me; I have lost relationships with women whose energy can never be duplicated or experienced by me ever again and I'm supposed to accept this pain and move on? I am a firm believer in the universe and the fact that everything that happens to us is meant to happen and all a part of our destiny. While I will admit a painless life with no struggle would be a bit boring, the pain received does not get any easier to handle.

Change breeds growth, growth breeds knowledge, and that knowledge breeds experiences. That is the formula of all our lives, no matter how different our lives are, this equation remains. I cannot say if the formula of life is truly meant to help all of us, but it all depends on your strength to deal with the hurdle's life tosses in your way. One of the hardest forms of change that I have experienced that hurts the deepest is the loss of friendships. Like I mention in the "FATHER" and "MOTHER" chapters, I have a bit of strained perception towards the idea of connecting with my family as a whole due to my relationship with my parents. So I always gravitated towards my friends and in turn they became the family that I always wanted, but the universe made sure to not include them in my life after a certain point. It could have been for the betterment of my existence, but it still does not get any easier to accept. As I am losing more and more people, I am starting to think it is for a specific reason that is way beyond my comprehension at this point. Life moves on whether I have answers to this question or not.

"Be the change you wish to see in the world" was always an interesting quote to me. We all have an idea of who we think we are, and I am sure most of us believe we are good humans at our core because we haven't done anything totally insane like commit murder, but I still question this common quote. I personally like to think that I am a perfect balance of good and bad, so that quote suggests to me that if I should be as good, nice, and respectful as possible in hopes that the version of the world I envision will follow suit, and I don't think that's possible and if somehow if it did that version of the world would be less entertaining. Humans will lie, cheat, steal, hurt, and fight each other till the end of the time, and although I am aware I can be a good person at times, I do indulge in that shitty side of the human condition at times and I don't think the change I would like to see is possible due to the negative behavior that is embedded into my DNA as well the bad behavior imbedded into the rest of the human race. Of course, we want the dark side of people's hearts to dissipate, but the yang cannot exist without the yin, so I always thought that quote sounds cool but not going to happen.

We cannot fight against our destines, all these moments are written for us so all we can do is adapt and accept the changes life throws our way. Friends will continue to come and go, relationships will continue to spark then fade, opportunities will continue to appear then disappear but at the end of the day, you have to remain intact and maneuver through it all if you want to get into the position of life you desire. Minor/major changes that occur in my life that are out of my "control" are initially the most terrifying moments I encounter but being blessed with the ability to adjust to new situations at a quicker rate helps me realign my focus on what's important sooner than later. All I can recommend to you is something that it took me a bit to accept as things changed for me; change will come as time flows and all you can do is accept, adjust, and reacclimate. Outside of the negative aspects of change that I experienced, even the good versions of change are still a scary reality to adjust to at first. Every new job I acquired on day one like clockwork, I was beyond nervous; the imposter syndrome kicks in and while I should have been overly excited for a new opportunity in life, I scared myself into submission. I have had times in life where the imposter syndrome was so hard to escape, I decided to quit a job before the chance of me losing the job ever got a chance to manifest. The fear of not being able to handle to change is very easy to absorb within but with the right amount of strength within it is just as easy to kick. Both sides of the pendulum of change that life has thrown my way has both benefited me and cause me to hold myself back. Do not be like that; accept, adapt, or forever remain locked into a submissive state your mind creates for you.

13-CONFIDENCE

13-CONFIDENCE

ACTUAL DEFINITION - THE FEELING OR BELIEF THAT ONE CAN RELY ON SOMEONE OR SOMETHING: FIRM TRUST

THE STATE OF FEELING CERTAIN ABOUT THE TRUTH OF SOMETHING.

MY DEFINITION - A FEELING THAT WE ALL HAVE INSIDE.HARD TO FIND. HARD TO MAINTAIN

I am an introverted, pessimistic, self-hating individual and while I still have the upmost confidence in myself and everything I do, everything I mentioned in the beginning of this sentence tends to overshadow that confidence at times and ultimately ends up pushing it deep down into my subconscious. I know I am worthy of everything I want out of this life but the battle between the optimism and pessimism rages on endlessly within my mind. My lack of confidence starts with my lack of results that satisfy me. Up until recently, around 2017 where I started acting on all the things I wanted to do in life and started manifesting what only lived in my head for so long is when the shift occurred. Prior to that, all I did was come up with good ideas and not do anything to make them become tangible, like this book you're holding for example. Until I flipped the switch in my brain to take ownership of my life and not let my negative thoughts lead the way is when this became more than a thought. In order for me to fully embrace the confidence within me, I constantly try to prove to myself that what I want can be mine if I work for it, results breed confidence within me. I am self-aware enough to know that things take time, but the time in between the work and result causes my pessimism to take over, which causes the confidence to deteriorate thus resetting the process in my mind. I have a lot going on in this head, huh? I am constantly trying to prove to myself that I can do everything my mind conjures, it is a never-ending war within this mind of mine. The disconnect between my heart, mind, and soul is the root of all the stoppage in my journey. My mind controls my heart and ends up poisoning my soul into a state of darkness and the confidence I did have. Confidence comes in waves dependent on whatever goal I am working towards specifically and what amount of experience I have with whatever I am working towards. Like some people, I'm sure the things we personally haven't manifested may seem like a fantasy prior to putting the work in to manifesting it but what I have noticed about myself as I've grown is that my willingness to try amongst all the confusion that clouds my mind created paired with my lack of confidence, I still at least try and see how things turn out. Aside from all the mental roadblocks I put up, I still end up trying. I still try even when the failure hurts and when the wins do not fully satisfy me. I still try and that should be enough, but I have a hard time convincing my mind that it is. I encourage anyone who is slightly like me in this scenario to just try and see what the fuck happens. It can and will hurt at times but just see and find out. That is the true definition of having confidence, I guess. Maintaining it when you get it is hard. So what do you do? Well, what I do to maintain my confidence in the things I am working to manifest when I feel myself about to spiral? I repeat at nauseam "everything will be okay" both out loud and in my head to force my mind to believe that things will work out and it does work SOMETIMES. Repeating those simple words creates a calming state within, it has worked most times but not all. What works for me is not guaranteed to work for you, but you're more than welcome to adapt this practice. Other times, I try to detach myself from my mind and the world around me by closing my eyes and by taking deep breaths. Having my eyes closed shut forces me into a state where I just try to lock my focus on my goal and block everything that stops me from reaching it. This method is still a work in progress but has worked once so I decided to adapt it to my routine. Lastly, I force my mind to a conclusion that I have no other choice in life but to do these things. I take away all options for myself, so I literally force myself into a state that is meant to cause my confidence flare up a bit but it's a case-by-case situation depending on what I am attempting. I take away my choice of not having confidence and push myself to believe my life depends on it, an extreme method that rarely works but it is all I got.

Confidence in yourself can be manifested from encouragement from others as well. Genuine, consistent encouragement, and friendships exist but they come in your life (in my experience) in small doses. If you have a support system who constantly reminds you of how great you are, you'll eventually start to believe (especially if you're not as pessimistic as me). So if you have those type of people in your life, listen to them and appreciate them.

My mind plays tricks on me constantly and tells me that I am not good enough or that everything I am doing will not work out in my favor, but I still move forward. My confidence, although not on the forefront of my thoughts regularly, still fuels me and exists me deep down at my core. I try to utilize it to its maximum potential before it goes back into hiding. Believe in yourself as much as you can. Through the power of manifestation, I learned that is impossible, you just must show yourself that it is true, other examples can only cut it for so long. Capture your confidence. If you were wondering (but probably aren't surprised) I had zero confidence coming into the process of starting this book but now that I am done I am confident the purpose I set for myself will be achieved once it reaches more

hands outside of the ones it is in currently. I say that confidently.

14-CONTROL

ACTUAL DEFINITION - THE POWER TO INFLUENCE OR DIRECT PEOPLE'S BEHAVIOR OR THE COURSE OF EVENTS

MY DEFINITION – THE POWER TO INFLUENCE OR DIRECT OUR BEHAVIOR AND THE COURSE OF OUR LIFE. WE HAVE THE POWER TO CONTROL WHERE WE END UP IN LIFE, WE JUST HAVE TO BE STRONG ENOUGH TO BELIEVE THAT

Control is not an illusion and it took me so long to realize this and say this confidently. In my life, I have consistently never taken accountability for anything that has gone wrong. I would always say things like "it was out of my control" or "It wasn't my fault; I couldn't control this!" and I learned this type of language is completely false and dismissive of any form of accountability. No person is bound to any contract in this life; what you want to do can be done if you have the strength within your mind to believe you can. For me, what helped achieve this mindset and change the definition of control was when I actually began manifesting the goals I contained in my mind. From goal one and starting this book and having it become a tangible piece of art, I literally proved to myself if I locked in and put the work in, I can shape my destiny in a way I could have never imagined. Results breed confidence in every step I made. Consistency breeds a resume of manifestation. For me, as I collected a plethora of memories of things I accomplished that started off as thoughts, it solidified my belief that as long as I remain in control of what thoughts enter my mind and what actions I take, anything is TRULY possible if you try.

Every decision we make, we control the outcome from beginning to end and what happens in between those moments, whether they dismantle your expectations or not, they shouldn't be looked at as anything more than a lesson to help shape the next situation you will ultimately be placed in. Through "failure" and "losses", I learned that they are nothing more than tools that are meant to aid my growth. The power of the tongue knows no bounds, so what you say both in a form of positive and negative speech is being heard by the universe always. So be mindful of what you say. Always. Even when you are typing something on social media, be careful what you say; not just out of fear of what the moderators of the site will say, but for the fear of what type of energy you will receive back. I truly believe every medium of communication we engage with has some form of universal influence floating in the background, so be mindful. The only guaranteed outcome in this life that we cannot control is death and although that guarantee exists every single day, everything leading up to that point is on you. So, do what you can to maneuver through the life in the most enjoyable way as you can till the end. Move with the awareness of the end but do not have your mind stuck on that thought. Control is an illusion; nothing happens in our life without our influence, so be mindful of your power. If I read what I just wrote when I was younger, I am SURE the trajectory of my path would have been filled with more light.

Enjoy the good and bad moments that occur and move with the awareness you are the one in charge.

15-COURAGE

15-COURAGE

ACTUAL DEFINITION - THE ABILITY TO DO SOMETHING THAT FRIGHTENS ONE

STRENGTH IN THE FACE OF PAIN OR GRIEF

MY DEFINITION - COURAGE IS THE MAGIC THAT TURNS DREAMS INTO REALITY

My definition of the word courage is a quote from a video game character from the RPG (role playing game for the unaware) called Tales of Symphonia: Dawn of The New World (long ass weird ass title I know) by the name of Richter Abend who is speaking to his very timid, shy, and weak pupil Emil, a character who I saw a lot of myself in that moment when this cutscene occurred for the first time. Till this day it resonates in my heart. For as long as I can remember I lacked courage to do things in life out of fear. The fear of putting my all into something and having it not working out how I envision crippled me many of times. The fear of failing combined with the fear of judgement from others eliminated any bit of courage I could think to conjure and ultimately held me back a lot. I still dial back to that way of thinking nowadays, but that magic that courage conjures, the power to turn your dreams into reality is real and I learned all I had to do was try and work my ass off no matter what type of negative thoughts fill my mind. It is really easier said than done. I have no blueprint on how to do this or even when I got the courage to try but when I did it felt refreshing and I felt comfortable with the possibility of failing. I got tired of holding myself back and started to continuously ask myself why I am fearing something that may never happen, I got tired of detouring the plans I had for myself and that's when the courage kicked in and took control of my thought process. I worked as hard as I could until my energy and motivation was exhausted every chance I got. This is an occurrence that happens more often now than what it was like for me when I was younger. The feeling of fear becomes exhausting to endure after a while, it reached a certain point I learned to work against it rather than let it guide me. I have proved to myself many of times that if you dream it you can achieve it and all you have to do is try to stuff the doubt down as far down as you can in order to progress. I have learned that the amount of courage that you maintain is dependent on the level of seriousness you have about going towards your dreams. If you have any hesitation when moving forward, you won't have any confidence when you decide to take that first step and will ultimately get you to end up taking two steps backward into an isolated state of no progression and confusion. I have lived in both realms of the spectrum, being filled with a massive amount of courage paired with an overwhelming amount of fear has left me in many of isolated states and what has worked for me is not guaranteed to work for you. Developing your own way out of doubt lies in the amount of belief that you have in the thought that it is possible to move forward. Lack of courage breeds an impassable state of isolation, so unless you enjoy that version of life and intend not to adjust I suggest you dig within as deep as possible and find the courage to progress and maintain it for as long as you can. It is possible all you must do is try. Courage is the magic that turns dreams into reality, do not forget that.

16-CRITICISM

16-CRITICISM

ACTUAL DEFINITION - THE EXPRESSION OF DISAPPROVAL OF SOMEONE OR SOMETHING BASED ON PRECIEVED FAULTS OR MISTAKES

THE ANALYSIS AND JUDGEMENT OF THE MERITS AND FAULTS OF A LITERARY OR ARTISTIC WORK

MY DEFINITION - UNWANTED BUT NECESSARY AT TIMES

I do not like criticism at all. I especially do not appreciate, enjoy, or need criticism from individuals who have zero experience in what they are criticizing me on. In my (slightly warped) mind, the criticism that is sent my way from an individual who hasn't tried what I am attempting is coming from a place of negativity and even jealousy in some cases and that type of energy is not allowed in my space, ever. On the flip side of criticism, there are individuals who offer criticism from a place of genuineness and only want to help rather than hinder your progress and while that type of feedback still stings just as bad as the negative kind, it allows me to internalize what they are saying and potentially apply it to my work rather than let it go in one ear and out the other. Both forms of criticism are inescapable and should be absorbed to a certain level. They should only be indulged in if it is coming from an informed, experienced, and genuine individual in certain amounts.

Too much may take you away from your zone of focus and may ultimately bring you to a space where those opinions dictate how you live/create. For me personally, I am my biggest critic and the type of feedback I present myself is (unfortunately) usually on the negative end of the spectrum. I beat myself up no matter how much positive feedback I get on anything I do, and I think I figured out why. I beat myself up consistently because I feel if I indulge in the positive side of the feedback it will get to my head and I will end up halting my progress rather than propelling it further. Let me explain. When things go my way consistently, I develop a mindset of invincibility. I believe in myself so much I know deep down that the heights I achieve are bound to happen and when it does happen I settle into the victories so much I tend to not work as hard and eventually that morphs into complacency. To avoid that roadblock, I beat myself up consistently and avoid the acknowledgment of my wins in hopes that I will be able to maintain the momentum I have so I can in turn use that as fuel to put towards achieving the bigger goals/dreams. I will admit this level of thinking is a bit nuts, but it has worked for me thus far and like they say, "if it isn't broke, don't fix it." After writing that out, I have another clear example of what I would like for you reader to do the opposite of, acknowledge your wins, accept the criticism you will receive in life and apply it to your life in any way you can that will aid you in your journey. As for me I expect tons of criticism on this book, it scares me, fuels, and motivates me all in the same breath but I know it will never compare to the things I have said in my own head about my art/self and that conjures an odd sense of peace in the madness for me. I also felt if I lived in a version of the world where everything I did got nothing but praise I know I would feel extremely uncomfortable so with that thought I look forward to the criticism with a healthy amount of fear on the side. Criticism is inevitable so the choice is yours to decide if you want to let it go in one ear and out the other or allow it to go in one ear and let it settle within your mind and lead it back out the other ear into a new form of energy that can be used to enhance your art rather than harm it.

17-DEPRESSION

17-DEPRESSION

ACTUAL DEFINITION - FEELINGS OF SEVERE DESPONDENCY AND DEJECTION

MY DEFINITION - A CURABLE CURSE IF YOU FIGHT

I have battled with depression for the entirety of my existence. I will probably battle with it for the rest of my life but when I developed the mind state that it was possible to not just live with it but fight against it as well I feel the trajectory of my life skyrocketed. The most solidified memory I have of when I think I first experienced depression is when I realized I was not like everyone I was around in my group of friends; I did not have a father. That realization was very hard to adjust to, especially when I would see the healthy relationships, they had with both of their parents. I was jealous. Certain friendships I consciously ended because I could not bear to consistently see what I wanted. My relationship with depression is so intense that whenever I find myself trapped in that darkness it bleeds out and affects everything else in my life from my performance at work, my focus, my appetite, my relationships with friends and family, literally everything gets affected, and if I am being honest my depression has ruined some of those things permanently. I have lost jobs due to my depression causing me to work less and even not show up some days. My depression and the distance I put in between myself and certain relationships I have had in the past, caused those relationships to crumble faster than they began. I have let my depression suffocate me so much, I began to indulge in many things I really should not have with the hope the depression would disappear. Marijuana and alcohol were the main mediums I utilized and as you could guess, they did not help at all. The last and most dangerous point of where my depression brought me to were the constant thoughts and attempts at suicide. The only method of suicide I was truly committed to was when I was at my lowest after a losing a job and I forcibly held a knife to my chest with the goal of sticking it directly through my heart but my fear of committing the act stopped me at the last second. That same night, I ended up falling asleep with the knife by my side with a tear-soaked pillow. Just in case if I ever got the courage to go through with the act again. I slept with that very same knife under my pillow to avoid any trips to the kitchen and questions any of my family might have for me if they ever saw me grab it. My depression has been nothing but a terrible influence on my life it has even eliminated memories of my youth. I do not remember much of anything in my life before my freshman year in high school. From the years 2010- 2016 all I knew was depression.

Those memories will never return because of the severity of my depression but who knows maybe it is for the best. Being cursed with depression back then felt (and still till this day sometimes) feels like this feeling will never go away, the feeling of being down for a reason you sometimes can't explain or not being able to control feels horrible. My suicidal thoughts have subsided since my last attempt and I have not had an attempt/have a knife under my pillow in a long while, but I sometimes fear those thoughts will come back. I've done and I am actively doing what I need to do to keep myself free from my depression, but it still is very much alive inside me and I don't know if I will ever reach a point where it will be gone forever but I try my best to keep going and not give up. Depression is a war that requires many battles to completely be over with and I encourage everyone who shares this same curse as me to know that you will have a bad day but the next isn't guaranteed to emulate the last one. Each day is a battle, and you need to do whatever you can to come out victorious. Just waking up is a victory in itself, having the opportunity to make these changes in your life and become a better you are a win, and you should feel honored and proud you're still here. I am still doing what works for me to keep my mind healthy and myself free from depression and I can't provide you with all the techniques that I do for me because it won't work for you unfortunately so what I recommend is to find, develop, and expand upon practices that make you feel comfortable enough to keep you free from the darkness and do them as much as you can until you feel secure within your existence. Do not give up, the process is very frustrating at times and it is a slow burn, but it is possible. If there is one thing, I do not want taken away from this chapter is the thought that what works for me will work for you. You must thoroughly analyze yourself and figure out what works for you in order to bring YOU peace. Do literally everything you can to bring yourself peace and the curse of depression will be lifted slowly each time you do. Take care of and protect your mental health at all costs; your life depends on it. Being depressed is just a feeling, it does not define your character as whole.

18- DESTINY

ACTUAL DEFINITION - THE EVENTS THAT WILL NECESSARILY HAPPEN TO A PARTICULAR PERSON OR THING IN THE FUTURE.

My DEFINITION - WE ALL ARE BORN WITH ONE AND ITS OUR LIFES MISSION TO DISCOVER WHAT OURS IS

When the word destiny comes to mind, the images that enter my mind are ones of lifelong goals being obtained, triumph, and victory. Images such as reaching the top of mountain after an exhausting journey from the bottom, winning a championship boxing match that you trained one year in preparation for, finally finishing that book you spent four plus years procrastinating and finally typing that last word and closing your laptop until you're ready to write the next one, becoming a bestselling author. When I think of destiny, I see things like this in my mind. A few of those things I see I clearly see for myself. The accomplishment of tasks that you set for yourself and pour your all into and having whatever type of victory you have in mind be your reality. That's destiny to me; that's what I feel we all want for ourselves at the end of the day, to be/have what we deem successful. Happiness is the goal. Focus, determination, ambition, and belief are all a part of the formula to manifesting our destinies. Without one of them, the darkness that our mind creates will cause us to lose our way to the top. If it wasn't apparent up till this point in the book, I have lost my way many of times and still do till this day, but I know for a fact I am here for reason. I know my destiny will be manifested because I wake up every day with air in my lungs and blood pumping in my heart - if I wasn't meant to feel I wouldn't be blessed with either. My destiny doesn't include a unanimous victory over the reigning champion of the boxing title, I sure hope it doesn't include me scaling a tall ass mountain because I am afraid of heights, but I do know every piece of art I create starting with this book and everything long after this will last the test of time and never be forgotten. I know this book will bring me to bestselling status. My destiny is to be so happy and so at peace that my mind will be silent and devoid of any stress or darkness. My destiny is to manifest the light that is inside my heart and have it shine bright endlessly externally so that it dissolves the darkness that is up here in this brain. My destiny is to be free from depression forever. I crave that. I need that. I will have that. I have all that, my physical body is just catching up. Manifest your destiny. We were all born with one and it takes TIME to figure out what yours is and you must be comfortable with that fact. Manifest your destiny, you want to be happy, don't you?

19- DO

ACTUAL DEFINITION - PERFORM (AN ACTION, THE PRECISE NATURE OF WHICH IS UNSPECIFIED)

MY DEFINITION - EVERYTHING YOU WANT YOU CAN HAVE IF YOU...DO

I overthink A LOT. My mind creates realities that end up stopping my progress and has probably held me back from some amazing opportunities (or protected me from some bullshit) but the fact of the matter is, if I got out of head and moved forward, my life would be way more pleasant than the version of it I created in my head. Most of the time, people don't "do" out of fear of the results not turning out how they have it formed in their head and end up not moving at all and the only advice I could give if I was ever asked to provide some is the kind that was given to me (and still repeated till this day) and that is to breathe and tell yourself this. Tell yourself that nothing in this life is ever a loss only a lesson at nauseum. Such a cliché I know but going back to the chapter titled "Control" the reality we shape is up to us. DO-ing stuff a necessary part of life, literally nothing we desire will manifest unless we put our best foot forward and put the work in. So why don't people "do"? Like I mentioned, I did not because my mind and soul conflicted, and the fear manifested but why else? Laziness.

Some people (myself included) don't have the drive to work all the time and they come up with 11 different reasons why what they are striving towards is too hard/ not possible to accomplish. Getting out of our heads and DO-ing is the only way win. It took a lot of time for me to learn this, but I eventually did. I am not preaching, and I am definitely not trying to force my mentality onto whoever is reading this. I am just presenting the facts that have applied to my life in a direct way the same way it was done for me. Although this information is super cliché and has been regurgitated into the ecosystem in many different forms the goal is to potentially breed more DO-ers. If I did not decide to "DO", you would not be reading this right now. The quote "good things come to those who wait" should not be interpreted as sitting around till what you want out of life falls into your lap. You must direct all the effort and time you have available towards your goals and "DO" everything you can to get what you want. So good things come to those who "DO" wait but that time waiting must be paired with time spent working. "DO" what you can when you can and wait patiently during that process because it will come to you eventually. I had to learn everything I just said, and I still need this reminder regularly so just know this isn't just preachy, cliché advice giving, it's another reminder that your author is learning, trying, and growing with each new chapter you indulge in.

20- DREAMS

ACTUAL DEFINITION - A SERIES OF THOUGHTS, IMAGES,AND SENSATIONS OCCURING IN A PERSON'S MIND DURING

A CHERISHED ASPIRATION, AMBITION, OR IDEAL

MY DEFINITION- OBTAINIABLE, TANGIABLE, POSSIBLE

This book was once a dream of mine. Every time I thought about this book, I craved the feeling of knowing what it felt like to have this be a reality. I craved the feeling of knowing people enjoyed my work and after four long years, this whole process was worth it. I dreamt of having the thought that I worked my ass off so hard and so consistently that I ended up having a book that I wrote with my own hands that would be sitting on someone's coffee table/nightstand/bookshelf and will be a part of their collection of reading material for years on end. I dreamt of being an Amazon/New York Times bestselling author, and while I am not at the time of me writing this, I will be after this is out. Crazy to think about, let alone write out but if being that you are reading this that means my dreams are one step closer to being a reality. Dreams manifest in our minds as a series of thoughts, images, and sensations that will remain nothing more than that if we do not pour all our energy into making those dreams become a reality. Depending on what your dreams are, the roads that need to be traversed to manifest them are either longer or shorter depending on the amount of work you put in. I have learned dreams require a few components that are crucial to your success and their manifestation. Those components are focus, faith, motivation, determination, and a positive attitude. Without any of these you are destined to a life of endlessly dreaming about the things that could have become a reality if you tried. For a long time, I found it very difficult to focus on one thing specifically, everything from school to sports I found to be extremely easy and with that bred boredom. I would never fully indulge in an interest because I was able to master it within minutes and I felt further indulging would be a waste of my time. I needed to feel challenged in order to stay focused. It was not until I decided to sit and write a 200+ page book did I ultimately feel focused enough to commit to one task. If you are one of those people who were diagnosed with A.D.H.D and told that your lack of focus is due to a medical condition, don't believe that. In my opinion you are, a highly intelligent and gifted individual who isn't being challenged. Garnering and maintaining the motivation to work towards my dreams is probably the hardest part of my journey. Like I mentioned previously, I can be extremely lazy at times and that paired with an overthinking nature, I cripple myself into submission. I do not know how to give words of wisdom on how to conjure motivation because I have not grown in that aspect. I recommend you do what I am not good at and learn to be patient with yourself and not beat yourself up when you are not productive when you feel you should be. Your dreams are not going anywhere. Faith and determination go hand in hand and the amount of belief you have in each of them is dependent your level of confidence. My struggle with confidence came from the lack of understanding of myself paired with no love for who I am. As I have grown to be a bit nicer to myself my confidence in every strep, I take has increased drastically. Cultivate love for yourself, genuine love, and your belief in yourself will be endless. I wish I knew all of these things when my dreams were nothing more than a series of thoughts, images, and sensations but alas I had zero focus and belief in myself and what I was doing for a very long time. Even till this day even after manifesting this book that is in your hand (that really isn't at the time I'm writing this) and a few other goals I set for myself I still struggle with maintaining that focus, determination, motivation, faith, belief ,and positive attitude. Ultimately at my core, I believe in myself more than I believe in the negative narrative my mind tries to create at times, so I do my best to just fight through it and keep moving forward relentlessly. Dreams do not have to be dreams forever. It is really your choice ultimately and the pace of the manifestation is dependent on how bad you want those dreams to come true. Most times we get inspired to do something because we saw someone before us manifest the same dream and I can promise you the person you are admiring was once you, a dreamer. So, there is nothing that separates them from you, if they can do it you can too if you really believe you can, all you have to do is put in twice as much as work them. Just know the path they traveled to get there is unique to them and CANNOT be emulated. Walk your own path and figure out what works best for you to get those dreams manifested. If only I could go back and have my younger self read this chapter, he would not be as lost as he was if he did. Dream, work, believe, manifest. Knowing what you want is half the battle so do the other half and put the work in and manifest those dreams of yours.

21- EMOTIONAL

ACTUAL DEFINITION - RELATING TO A PERSON'S EMOTIONS

AROUSING OR CHARACTERIZED BY INTENSE FEELING

(OF A PERSON) HAVING FEELINGS THAT ARE EASILY EXCITED AND OPENLY DISPLAYING

MY DEFINITION - TABOO AMONGST MEN FOR SOME REASON, ESPECIALLY IN THE BLACK COMMUNITY. ME.

I AM AN EMOTIONALLY INTELLIGENT INDIVIDUAL. I CRY ALOT. I HAVE NO PROBLEM EXPRESSING HOW I FEEL EVER. IM SENSITIVE AS FUCK. DID I MENTION I CRY A LOT? Now that all of that is out of the way let us proceed. Being expressive with my emotions has always been so easy for me as opposed to other black men who were a part of my life and in my community. Growing up I would hear things like "don't be a bitch" or "boys don't cry" and being that I did the opposite of my behavior, I was shunned upon by everyone except the women in my life. They taught me it is okay to react emotionally as long as you are being authentic with them and can learn to rationalize when is the time to be emotional and when is the time to be logical. I was just naturally gifted with the ability to feel everything that invades my consciousness, even situations that do not affect me directly trigger my empathetic side and cause me to feel for others and even cry for them, As far back as my youthful days and even more so now, I have accepted this side of me and even though I come from a community where the alphas tried to tell me there was something wrong with me I still live this way unapologetically. I call myself an emotional alpha these days; those alpha traits are synonymous with my ego. So while it is present, I dial back to my emotional side more often. The statement, "boys don't cry", is truly one of the most toxic statements in existence. Forcing a boy to maintain his toughness throughout every situation he encounters slowly damages his psyche and their ability to connect as they grow. Their perception of the world becomes very black and white and eliminates their ability to be empathetic. It is not fair to them and the other people they will encounter on their journey. Being as emotional as I am, I'm sure it's tough for the people in my life to deal with at all times and I am cognizant of that fact, but I literally can't help but to express how I feel in any and every situation. There are no secrets with me. You will always know how I feel. In certain relationships I've had with women I have been told that I am the "girl" in the relationship and that was one of the most triggering and confusing sentences that ever went into one ear and out the other. As a collective we need to stop making traits and habits being gender specific. Before we had these titles like "men "and "women" we were all humans who felt both

similarly and differently but the unseen connection between us

emotionally was always present. Before communication with words,

emotions were the only means of connecting with one another. I feel

these societal standards separated us but that is for a different book

entirely. Back to me being a crybaby and shit.

The one thing that is guaranteed to make me cry every time (besides

failure) is seeing any form media depicting a dog being injured/killed.

Just writing that got me teary eyed. I love dogs more than anything.

They are such loyal and majestic creatures who do not deserve any

type of pain in my eyes (yes even Cujo or the dog from the sandlot).

The first time I remember really getting a dog induced cry is the

movie, I Am Legend, with Will Smith when his partner and dog

Samantha are attacked by the dark seekers (creatures in the film) and

ultimately killed due to Will smiths character having to break her neck

before she gets fully infected. Till this day, no matter how much I love

this movie, I cannot watch it because the emotions will flare up. I am

emotional and I own that side of me and if you don't you should or you

will miss out on a whole different level of communication and

frequency you can experience with the ones around you. It is okay to

be sad. It is okay to cry. Fellas you don't need to be tough all the time, let your guard down once and awhile and be vulnerable with your partner and hopefully the people around you won't judge you - and if they do you do not need them. One important lesson I learned from a previous relationship with a Taurus was to balance logic with my emotions. If you are unaware based off what I read online, it says that most Taurus tend to think more logically than emotional, and my ex-girlfriend (thankfully) taught me the skill to balance my emotional and logical takes on life. We had to get through a lot of back and forth in order for me to understand because I was so stuck in my emotional side, but it worked out, after we broke up. I had no room in my brain to actually hear or understand what she was trying to tell me back then, but I finally got it and I am eternally grateful for her contribution to my life. This is the only relationship I have been in where I wish I could go back, where I wish I was the best version of myself to make things right between us. This is the only person I only thought to marry. I am eternally grateful for the Taurus. I had to do a lot of digging on the inside to fully understand and accept how my emotional side doesn't just affect me but there is indeed a bleeding effect that invades the people around me both positively and negatively. I try to be more aware of this fact in current day, but I will still cry first chance I get.

So, while yes, it IS totally fine to be in tune with your emotions sometimes in life (especially entrepreneurs) you must have a logical approach to a situation in order to move forward. Make sense of your emotions and do not deny them. Ever.

22- ESCAPE

ACTUAL DEFINITION - BREAK FREE FROM CONFINEMENT OR CONTROL

FAIL TO BE NOTICED OR REMEMBERED NY (SOMEONE)

MY DEFINITION - A HEALTHY NECESSITY, A NECESSARY OUTLET, FREEDOM

Sometimes we need to get away. The realities of our reality are sometimes too harsh to endure and a break from the bad, and even the good, is another key that can be used to unlock the door to happiness. In some way we are all tightly chained by our realities whether it's through our work, art, families we all (hopefully) have relationships to maintain and things to take care of but what do you do when you need to get away from all that? I can only speak for what works for me and even though I am an overthinking, hardworking individual, I really do try my best to provide myself with many different forms of escape that put me at peace that I will share in a second but first I want you as the reader to take a second to put your bookmark in, close your eyes for a brief moment and think of what forms of escape that you have in your life. If you do not have one, think of something you can apply to your life before you continue reading this book. I think it is important that we all have something that we indulge in to free us from our responsibilities and struggles that life throws our way. We all deserve that level of peace especially those of us who have a strong work ethic, we need that mental stillness as well as the physical relaxation, especially if we want to continue to maintain the ability to be able to work towards and expand upon our goals.

I do have a hard time stopping but while pushing forward on my journey I managed to garner a few escapes from the struggles that life rolls my way that I love to and need to utilize often in order to keep myself as centered as possible. One escape being the gym. I recall my interest with working out started in high school for a superficial reason. Instead of a typical gym class with dumb activities and sports we had the option of attending the weight room and that's usually where all the girls went so naturally I went where they did in hopes of getting their attention (which I never got) and to potentially impress them with my strength that I didn't have. My interest in working out was solidified in my freshman year of college when I got called "too skinny" too many times by too many attractive women I decided the last time that happened was the last time and was the moment when I decided to make a change and shape my body into something more appealing. My interest in working out started out as such a surface level reasoning but quickly shaped into a consistent part of my routine and ultimately became about making myself feel good rather than impressing the girls. I focused on me and I began liking what I saw and till this day I try to work out no less than three times a week, the peace it provides no bounds. There is something so relaxing about putting your headphones up at maximum volume with your favorite playlist on and going to work in the gym. Deadlifts and pull ups are my favorite exercises, they bring me so much joy. The escapism the gym provides is probably my healthiest escape I have and makes me the happiest except when I am in pain after an intense workout. Every second of it is worth it. Another escape that I have had since I was a kid with no siblings were/are video games, specifically RPGS. (Role Playing Games) Do not judge.

Till this day, I cannot resist indulging in a good RPG. The long journeys, the in-depth characters, the captivating battle systems, the beautiful worlds, the soothing music, it really gets no better than that. RPGs are typically longer games with full stories that provide backstories to large worlds and larger casts of characters and as these games go on you can't help but to be captivated by the experience and for me I get lost in it so deeply I get attached to these characters. Maybe this is my way of coping with not having anyone to play with? Who knows but I genuinely cannot help but to indulge in these games even till this day. They are consistently stress relievers and although video games are looked down upon as childish outlets the older you get to the majority of society. Or as an unhealthy medium, I believe anything in moderation is fine for you, especially if it makes you happy. I say all this to say find what brings you peace from the realities of your reality and find something that will reduce the weight off your shoulders and not add to them. I had to learn to be okay with the routes I was given, I had to learn to accept what lead me towards peace. I let societies standards dictate what should bring me peace. I let other opinions shape my mediums for peace. For a while I compared my outlets to others, I felt mine weren't as cool or entertaining, but I had to realize what's for me, is for me and what I am good at and what I enjoy is not going to have the same effect for someone else. I embraced my interests. I accepted my outlets. There are so many escape routes you can take that will lead you towards a better tomorrow, you are not limited to one road, so pick one and move forward as fast as you can. FIND AN ESCAPE ASAP.

23- FAMILY

23-FAMILY

ACTUAL DEFINITION - A GROUP CONSISTING OF PARENTS AND CHILDREN LIVING TOGETHER IN A HOUSEHOLD

ALL THE DESCENDANTS OF A COMMON ANCESTOR

MY DEFINITION - NECESSARY, HELPFUL, A BLESSING, LOVING, NURTURING, EVERYONE ISN'T LUCKY ENOUGH TO HAVE ONE UNFORTUNATLEY

For starters, I would like to say I am eternally grateful and honored to have a family. So many do not have a family to call their own for a bunch of different sad reasons (being disowned, abortion, death at birth, divorces etc etc) but the fact that I was given the honor to have one that loves me so much means the world to me and I do not take it for granted. My family is relatively small for reasons I can only guess. Some family members are in jail, others are dead, and some we just have never associated with for different reasons that I was never told even till this day (I guess I could ask) but I would say the total number of my family members will count up to 9 people. To some of you, that may not compare to the amount you have and to others this may be a surprising and larger amount than the total you have, but no matter the amount as long as the relationship is intact that's all that matters in the end. I say that but my relationship with my family is not as perfect and stable as I would like it to be and I honestly do not know why. The most traumatic thing that I can think of that has affected me family wise is my father not being present and him abandoning my mother and I, but the immediate family I have; on paper everything has been fine. The only other thing I can think of is the passing of my grandfather, a lot changed after that I noticed. We weren't the richest or the poorest, but we always had what we needed, I attended all levels of school and was even given the opportunity to go to college (that I didn't fully take advantage of) and they have always been in my corner no matter the situation, so why isn't our relationship as strong as it should be? I literally have no idea and it is something I actively have been trying to figure out for myself. I am the only introverted member of my family so as I sat with my family during the holidays growing up I noticed early on that I am nothing like the rest of them, it became a bit uncomfortable for me to even be around them at times because the differences are so apparent. Being the black sheep was an empowering and super weird feeling simultaneously and in turn made me more comfortable being alone and doing my own thing rather than spending time and actually getting to know the members of my family.

The concept of time looms over my brain when I take the time to acknowledge it and remind myself that we are not here forever. When I have these thoughts, it makes me want to break that disconnect with my relationship with my family and actively try to spend time and get to know them more but it's very hard for me to break that comfort wall I built for myself. I feel it stems from the awkward relationship I have with my mother. We didn't spend a whole lot of time growing up, mostly because she worked a lot (providing for me) and that paired with not having a dad, I feel subconsciously I developed some form of resentment that morphed into disassociation with all of my family. The fact that I am aware of all this and not making an active effort to change this is an issue I keep presenting in front of myself and I will change eventually but unfortunately I am stuck in the mold of moving at my own pace and not with a sense of urgency. The last thing I want for myself is any form of regret/wishes for time spent, so that is one of my motivations going forward in life that will be achieved. I would like to be the example of what not to be and how not to act with your family. Be as present as possible, be as interactive as possible with them because without them, you wouldn't be here and without them you wouldn't be who you are today so repay them by being in their corner the same way they have been for you. I say that to whoever is reading this while simultaneously saying this to myself. Let us acknowledge, process, and apply these words and establish/strengthen the relationships we have with them. We owe them that much. As I am growing, I am learning the relationship with your family is truly one of the most prized possessions you can hold and knowing that everyone is not blessed with the opportunity to have one with the fact that I do, makes me want to hold onto it as close as I can. I clearly have so much to work on internally before I can feel comfortable expanding upon that relationship. I am eternally grateful to have the opportunity to have a family. I do not take them for granted and in my own way, at my own pace I am eliminating the imbalanced (one sided) energy I have created that caused the distance between us.

24-FATHER

24-FATHER

ACTUAL DEFINITION - A MAN IN RELATION TO HIS CHILD OR CHILDREN

MY DEFINITION - SOMETHING I NEVER HAD BUT SOMETHING I WANNA BE AND WILL BE THE BEST AT.

Clarence Christopher Wilkins is the name of my father, the name of a man I never met, the name of a man who took the cowardice way out and abandoned my mother while pregnant with me. I hold a lot of resentment towards this man. When I was younger, you could classify my feelings as hate and disgust; now it can be labeled as indifferent and disappointment. For a long while, I held a lot of guilt for being alive; I felt like me being in my mother's womb was the reason why he left, and their separation was sped up because of me. I hated my existence whenever I had those thoughts. I never knew exactly what type of relationship they had, they could have been soulmates and my existence getting in the middle of a young couple in the 90s who had their whole lives ahead of them now they had to deal with some kid they didn't plan to have. Thinking these thoughts repeatedly may have been the start of depression. I felt so bad for existing at the time I could do nothing but embrace how I felt. The negative thoughts controlled the majority of my youth. Sometimes I feel if I had a say and had those thoughts before leaving the womb I probably would have chosen not to be born in order to allow them to flourish in life until they were actually prepared to have a child but alas here I am. This man, this Clarence Christopher Wilkins, the man who is technically my father, I have literally no idea where he is till this day and to be honest if I did know at this point in my life at age 28 I have no idea what I would do. I am a fully formed (bit broken) individual and I don't desire any kind of relationship with him and although I am not pressed for this information, it would be really cool to know why he left and where he's been and if he ever had any regrets. I do not crave that information but if I look outside myself for a second, I believe that is exactly what I need to further myself along my path towards healing and a depression free life. Who knows, and I honestly may never know but what I do know and what I would like other individuals reading this who have experienced something similar is that even though you are missing that parent you are not them. Because they committed such an emotionless and evil act that does not mean you will do the same. I want you to know any negative traits you hold or things that have happened to you in life that suck is not an extension of the abandonment by that parent, everything that happens is pre destined and meant to happen. For a while, I blamed everything on him, but I slowly learned accountability is also a necessary component to healing. I also used to attribute any negative part of my personality to him and blame him for having me inherit that side but also I had to realize that is also not true because I don't know anything other than his name, so I don't have anything to compare myself to other than myself. I assumed he is bad because he made a bad decision and who is to say I would not make the same decision if I was at the same crossroads. I am so ambitious I do not know what I would do. If you have the opportunity to meet and express how you feel to that parent, I would say do it, I personally would be very hesitant, but I know it wouldn't be a mistake. If you are not so lucky to have that opportunity I would say you should appreciate what parents/family you do have that are present in your life and try to embrace how they make you feel and not how you wish that absent parent would make you feel. Do not blame yourself for their absence you were meant to be here, and you deserve love from the ones who are by your side and not the ones who would up and leave with no remorse. Initially if I ever met this man I always joked that if he wanted a relationship with me I would fake it and just milk him for money until I had he had nothing left, and every time I told somebody that they always gave me the side eye and told me that it wasn't right. I did not agree for a long time but now I do. For so long I never took accountability for how I turned out and put most of the blame on a man I never met, and I would be just as bad if not worse than him if I committed to the idea of using him strictly for money. I had to travel a very steep learning curve in order to come to this realization so while I may have a bit of resentment in my heart for this man, I never met I have no hate. I am grateful to be here and thankful for his contribution to my existence. If I met Clarence Christopher Wilkins tomorrow, the first thing I would ask is why, then secondly say I appreciate your absence because if you stayed around your behavior may have corrupted my mind and turned me into who he is. I would like to think I turned out well without him and I hope you feel the same about yourself.

25-FLAWS

25-FLAWS

ACTUAL DEFINITION - A MARK, FAULT, OR OTHER

IMPERFECTION THAT MARS A SUBSTANCE OR OBJECT

MY DEFINITION - WE ALL HAVE THEM, FACE THEM, OWN

THEM, EMBRACE THEM. THEY AREN'T GOING ANYWHERE NO

MATTER WHAT YOU DO

"WE ALL HAVE THEM, FACE THEM, OWN THEM." If me from ages 10 -27 read this, I am SURE he would have a slightly better mental state. My hairline was gone at age 28 (luckily the bald head looks great on me) slight body dysmorphia around my forearm/wrist area, I'm a bad communicator, I assume and create realties that aren't real and last but certainly not least the, last "flaw" is my nose. It is big and long and my first noticeable "flaw" that was apparent to me with the help of a kid from my middle school by the name of Kyle Reeves. Is this what they call a blessing in disguise? Getting made fun of so much in your youth simultaneously helping make you more resistant to those comments in adulthood when things matter way more? Who knows, but these "flaws" bred a bunch of insecurities that still sit with me till this very day. Literally till this day whenever someone is sitting on the side of me (especially if they are extremely attractive) and my side profile is exposed, I do whatever I can to cover my cheek/nose with my hand, so they don't see and have the opportunity to make any jokes/judgements. Whether it is directly or indirectly I do not want either thrown my way. My insecurities are showing, I know. Going back to Kyle Reeves and kids like him who make fun of other kids all through school. I truly wonder if they remember these moments in school or develop any form of remorse or shame? Probably not.

People do not give a fuck about each other. That is for another chapter though. NOW back to my flaws and insecurities! These flaws that I grew familiar with truly shaped me into the insecure individual that I was in the past (and am at times today). It was truly an inescapable experience that I let get the best of me on many occasions. Being the butt of jokes on jokes bred thoughts of getting nose surgery and even more intense moments of me shoving my hand up against my nose using force with the only hope of getting it to shrink. I would even go as far to even force more sturdy objects like books and game cases against it. I hated it. None of my other family members have a nose like this, so why me? Prior to discovering any passions, I am sure if someone asked what I wanted out of this life more than anything I know for a fact I would say that I would want enough funds to get nose surgery. Till this day I still have those thoughts occasionally cross my mind, but they do not stay for too long. Having these 'flaws' embedded into my mind also in turn held me back from making connections with women and even the idea of breeding new friendships with other guys. As you get closer with a partner or a pal you get comfortable enough with each other to make jokes and because I was so used to getting jokes from a negative point of view I wasn't sure if I could even handle them from a space that meant no true harm, so I didn't interact as much and embraced being alone. As I am writing this, I am realizing my nose is my most triggering flaw and I never realized it till now. The other ones also affect my spirit, but I guess the amount of times they are triggered are not as often as this one. Heh.

As I got older and more comfortable in this vessel, I learned to live with these flaws rather than constantly fight against them and (dangerously) try to change them. Like my definition clearly says, these flaws are not going anywhere no matter how hard you try. Your perception of yourself may change slightly when you look in the mirror but to someone else, like your version of a Kyle Reeves in your life your nose or whatever will always be big or ugly so just try to remain sturdy doing those moments and try to at the very least to accept what you see in the mirror then grow to enjoy it over time. I do not believe mistakes were made when I was born, or when a kid is born with a missing limb, or another with down syndrome, these are not curses. They are blessings in disguise because they are part of the unique genetic makeup we possess; no matter where we turn, right or left, up or down you will never find someone in the world who is exactly like you. YOU ARE UNIQUE AND YOU ARE BEAUTIFUL. So, to the bully who tormented me in my youth and made me feel less than, I say these final words.

FUCK YOU, Kyle Reeves.

26-GRATEFUL

26-GRATEFUL

ACTUAL DEFINITION - FEELING OR SHOWING AN APPRECIATION OF KINDNESS. THANKFUL

MY DEFINITION - BE THIS EVERY SINGLE DAY IN EVERY SINGLE SCENARIO THAT PRESENTS ITSELF IN YOUR UNIVERSE

I have not always been the type to openly to express how grateful I am to be alive. Most days I wake up, go about my business, and continue my journey towards manifesting my destiny. I don't take much time to just slow down appreciate the opportunities that have been given to me from my family and the universe and I do not know why I am not outwardly grateful, but I strive to change that. I would not be here today without the wisdom and protection I have had from my family. The universe has blessed me for years and while I am aware of this, and yet I still don't express how grateful I am repeatedly. I do not take the time to thank them for it all. Internally I am so thankful and appreciative, but I've learned as I have grown that outward expression and appreciation is way more beneficial not just for me, but it is just as fulfilling for the ones I am communicating with, the universe included. Getting validation and appreciation feels great, coming from a person who rarely receives either, the times I have gotten them my day was made. The purpose of this chapter is not for you to put this book down and try to contact me personally and help me find out why I have trouble expressing how grateful I am, but my only intention is strictly to provide you with another example of what not to be like. I regret not being as outwardly grateful for everything I have in my life and if I can be the one to be the example of what not to be in order for others to have a better life; I will gladly accept that role. The regret I hold is partnered with fear, the fear of not getting the proper opportunity to express my gratefulness for everything that my mother and grandmother have given/taught me. While our relationships are currently still intact, and I still have the opportunity to make these relationships stronger I fear the amount of time I have left to do so isn't as long as I think it is. A very negative attitude I need to dismiss. The acknowledgement of mortality is crippling. You are probably asking, "what's so hard about picking up the phone and calling them if it's not too late?" Well that introverted overthinking nature still walks with me very closely. Even now as an adult I believe that plays a major role in my lack of gratefulness/scattered thought process to simple concepts. My motivation to try to express how grateful I am for them and everything they have done for me is extremely high deep down but the negative thoughts I have halt all attempts at progress. Know what is also paired with that with negativity? You guessed it- it is once again fear and although I know them, I know they love me and appreciate me, the fear of getting to know someone I feel is a stranger is a bit scary. My mind has convinced me it is too late, but my heart tells me it is not. The battle between my mind and my heart is ongoing but it will pass. I will develop the courage to have this conversation with my family and the universe and finally express how grateful I am for them and everything they have done, but until then, if you are in the complete opposite relationship with being grateful (I really hope you are), I encourage you to put the bookmark in for a second and communicate with your loved ones and tell them how grateful you are for them. Then when you are back in bed-or wherever you choose to read this-close your eyes and out loud express how grateful you are to be here to the universe (or what/whoever you believe in) and rinse and repeat as often as you can. I will start with these same practices and progress at my own pace, I am grateful to be here and I am eternally grateful for whoever is reading this with no judgement. I am grateful for those who have full acceptance of all the contents contained in this book that they have read thus far, no matter how scattered my thoughts come across or how lost I sound in each chapter. I am grateful for the days I continue to have air flowing in my lungs and blood pumping into my heart, without my mother I would not have either. I am eternally grateful for every experience I have had in life both good and bad it was all worth it and a necessary part of my growth. Be grateful,

eternally.

27- HABITS

27-HABITS

ACTUAL DEFINITION - A SETTLED OR REGULAR TENDENCY OR PRACTICE, ESPECIALLY ONE THAT IS HARD TO GIVE UP

MY DEFINITION - HARD TO GIVE UP, HARD TO BREAK BUT A NECESSARY ADJUSTMENT IF YOU WANNA ASCEND TO THE NEXT PHASE OF YOUR LIFE

I have a lot of annoying and bad habits that need to be broken in order for me to transcend to the next level of my life. I need to stop biting my nails when I get anxious; I need to stop procrastinating. I need to stop doubting myself; I need to stop assuming; I need to stop being judgmental. I need to break these habits, and a few more but where and how do I start?

I feel the obvious answer is to do the opposite of what I am already doing or do other things to replace those negative habits with positive alternatives and while both of those sound so much harder than they probably are, I still can't do it. As human beings we are creatures of habit and do things specifically catered towards our convenience, we do anything and everything to hold onto that or else (in our minds we think) everything will fall apart. If things go so "well" when these habits are not broken, and our lives are progressing how we want, then what is the point of making an adjustment - and if we try is it even possible/worth it? I have learned throughout my journey to not make time for my bad habits. To be so busy and to be so wrapped up into your passions where you literally have no time to distribute to anything but your work (healthy mediums only) you will notice time fly by and you will notice you haven't bitten one nail or judged a single individual. When I discovered my passions, I really took advantage of the blessing and actively tried my best each and every single day to expand upon and use them as a healthy distraction from the bullshit. FAR from perfect, but it works for me and I encourage anyone reading this to try this: work to manifest your passions at healthy pace regularly to the point where your bad habits have no room in your routine.

I'm aware some bad habits like biting nails and even smoking cigarettes require a bit more focus to get rid of, but the one thing that is NEEDED to break any habit and maintain your good ones is the strength/faith that you will be able to break those habits in half. You need the will and the confidence in yourself to be able to break them. Like anything in this life if you want it you must work for it. Super cliché but it is the truth, if you want to live a life (bad) habit free you need to do what works for you and do it religiously till you are free. My bad habits still very much play an active role in my life and even as dedicating more time things that are a healthy distraction I subconsciously still indulge in my bad habits, they are almost a part of my routine at this point, but I know it's possible to get rid of them. One day. Acknowledge everything in your life that you deem to be a flaw and slowly conjure healthy replacements in your routine with the belief that they will disappear eventually. Work with no faith is counterproductive, so if you notice these bad habits taking control and affecting your life in a counterproductive manner you to have patiently work towards getting the under control or gone forever. My bad habits still exist to this day and I have acknowledged them years prior to my desire to make any real change so know you are in for the long haul when you go about changing your life. What is the expression? "Rome wasn't built in a day" or something like that. Take that very cliché quote and replace Rome with "your life" and break those bad habits.

28-HATE

28-HATE

ACTUAL DEFINITION - FEEL INTENSE OR PASSIONATE DISLIKE FOR (SOMEONE)

MY DEFINITION - BEING HATED > HATING SOMEONE ELSE

I personally have never held a form of darkness in my heart where I could confidently say I hate someone. Even my relationship with depression has never caused me to express hate for myself and actually mean it. I have done things in my life that I can look back on and truly hate that I allowed myself to do, but I never once hated myself for those acts; just a bit disappointed that is all. I have consistently been educated and reminded of people in this world who are truly evil and probably deserve my hate, but I cannot bring myself to allow my heart to beat in that way. When it comes to my discomfort with someone's motives, intentions, and actions I just eliminate their existence from my mind completely. You cannot hate who does not exist right? Like I mentioned earlier, I have done things throughout my life that I am not proud of, but without me knowing for sure I am positive I have gained some form of hate from whoever I have wronged in my past. I have lied, stolen, and said some really harsh things to people who are no longer in my life and although I would like to hope there is no hate for me, it can't be helped if it exists; in most of those situations that occurred the hate is warranted. If it were possible to reverse my behavior, I would but I've come to realize who I was is not me at my core, so I try to not crucify myself too hard in the times I self-reflect on how I acted. If whoever I have done wrong is SOMEHOW reading this; first of all I commend you for purchasing this and indulging in this book enough to get to this chapter; I respect your commitment to your distaste for me but know I am truly sorry for what I have done something that cut you deeply internally.

My definition says that being hated is better than hating someone else which may contradict everything you have just read, but what I mean is the energy being spent to hate is extremely valuable. Our time here on Earth is limited, and for someone to waste that precious amount of time to direct nothing but hate towards you? Sounds like a complete waste if you ask me. The energy being spent to hate you will do nothing but propel you forward and stagger the hater. I also think being hated is better than hating someone else because (at least in my mind) it is a clear indicator that you are doing something right. No matter what you do in life or how successful we become we will always attract some haters for different reasons, such as your position in life may be "greater" than theirs or from their perception what you are doing is not as impressive compared to what they are doing. Whichever direction the hate goes, it has nothing to do with you and it should not deflect from your goals in life. Hate that is given is typically an extension of that person's lack of whatever they are directing their hate towards. Haters are always going to hate/exist. Embrace the hate. If you have it within you, at the very least you should try to apologize to the person if you actually did something wrong to warrant that hate. As the hippies say, "peace and love man". Also, another generic quote before we close this chapter. "Don't hate, appreciate."

29-HELP

29-HELP

ACTUAL DEFINITION -MAKE IT EASIER FOR (SOMEONE) TO DO SOMETHING BY OFFERING ONE'S SERVICES OR RESOURCES.

SERVE SOMEONE WITH (FOOD OR DRINK)

MY DEFINITION - HARD TO ACCEPT WHEN YOU'RE STUBBORN BUT NEEDED AT TIMES

There is no "I" in team or so say they say right? When you are a stubborn individual it is hard to ask - like it is really, REALLY hard to ask for help. Being independent with a hefty track record of getting things done and getting things when you want with your own resources, on your own time, with your own hands, it is difficult to convince yourself that help is ever an option in any scenario you may encounter. Having a group of friends/a stable family system at home guarantees you some help in situations if you need it and I personally have that, but I feel the main factor as to why I won't accept any help is my pride. I have done so much thus far on my own merit, sometimes I feel asking for any type of help would make me feel less of myself- and I do not like that feeling at all. I make myself feel that way more than enough times on my own, having an external force contribute to that feeling would further induce me with stress I don't need. Not much different from it coming strictly from me. Hypocritical I know. I know it is not weak to ask for help. It is not a bad thing to be helped. I am fully aware of these things, but my pride just will not let go. Being that I am an over-thinker. I play out the scenario in my head prior to asking for help, and what the person who I asked for help thinks of me - I usually think they will think less of me. If it was not even more apparent, my overthinking nature is embedded into my being. I am working through this I SWEAR. I am learning as I go, I am learning to recognize that breaking down the pride requires the same level of vulnerability I share when I am being expressive with my emotions, finding that healthy medium is hard but possible. If you're like me at all and have trouble asking for help, you know the discomforting feeling that goes down your spine when you even have the thought, but the fact of the matter is we all need help sometimes. We will not become successful entrepreneurs without a team. We will not get through sad moments without a shoulder to cry on. Why try to create a new reality on your own? Why? Pride is why.

How do we eliminate our pride/ego? I personally have not encountered any methods (I have heard that I should try more psychedelics one day) but letting your guard down, and just being vulnerable and open minded to something unfamiliar is really the only way. If you want anything in your life to change, you must choose to indulge in the new situations that may arise and adjust to them accordingly. It is funny how we will call for help only if its life threatening but not life altering. You do not know what may end up happening if you decide to get some help. It could potentially change your entire journey for the better. I am saying all this to you, the reader, but I am also speaking to myself in this moment. It is going to be hard to accept- hard to swallow the fact that your independence is tossed to the wayside and you are asking for help, but again like they say...there's no "I" in team. There is also no "I" in help either, you get the point (I hope). If you are lucky enough to be blessed with a community who are in your life regularly and genuinely care about your wellbeing know that help is always available to you and for you. For me, my community starts with my family then friends, I cannot count all the fingers and toes that I possess the amount of times they have helped me out when I was vulnerable enough to tuck my pride in my pocket and actually ask for assistance. It always stings no matter how many times you are down and out. Committing to the act of asking for help is a very hard adjustment for the independent but if you have the community in your corner who's willing to help, keeping

in mind that everyone isn't blessed with the opportunity I would say it's

a smart idea to toss the pride away and take advantage if you can

while you can. Never view help in a negative light. You were in a

position in life where you needed nothing but help just to function so if

you apply that same logic to your adulthood you will not lose.

30-INTROVERTED

30-INTROVERTED

ACTUAL DEFINITION - OF, DENOTING, OR TYPICAL OF AN INTROVERT

MY DEFINITION - ME AND PROBABLY YOU AS WELL AND THATS OKAY

"Why are you so quiet?" "Are you shy?" "You don't know how to talk?" "You are so awkward" "Are you okay?" Those are a small amount of questions/statements that have been tossed in my direction while I have been engulfed in my introverted nature in public settings. VERY ANNOYING. The common misconception of introverts is that we do not like to interact or are too shy to talk. This chapter is loosely committed to the idea of dissolving that stigma forever. Introverted individuals learn the value of their own space early on and appreciate the comfort in that space, and typically when we are off to the side or up against the wall at the party not talking we are having an enjoyable experience in the reality we created, that's all. Being the life of the party is not a desire for us, observing the life of the party is more appealing. Introverts are so misunderstood in society and I never understood why. In my mind introverts, are the most authentic humans you will encounter; we own the space we are in at all times and move how we want in those spaces and do what is best for us.

Even if that means not talking to anyone and just observing, that is what we will do. Introverts acquire comfort in solitude earlier than an extrovert does, so if plans are canceled for the evening, an introvert will thrive while the extrovert will be miserable. We won't conform to society's standards of communication and interaction, BUT that doesn't mean we hate you or anything (in most cases we don't but that could be the case). We just value our own peace way more than we value time interacting halfheartedly with you.

Another misconception about introverts is that we are not capable of being expressive with our emotions because we tend to be to ourselves more than we interact with the outside world, the perception is that we have a hard time connecting/empathizing. I am living proof that is not true at all. For me, I cannot help but to be expressive or else I will drive myself insane. I express how I feel when I feel, always. I have been known to overly express my emotions, that is how bad I am at filtering my truth. While my ability to express myself is unique to me, I am sure other introverts reading this would also have their own version of what I said. I'm not sure why people think this about us, and I believe we are more in tune with our energy/emotions than extroverts because we don't distribute our energy willingly, we are able to control the flow of our feelings because we do not willingly put ourselves in situations where they would be compromised.

As I have interacted more and grown, I have become able to lean more towards the ambivert side of life, but I still dial back to the introverted side more often than the communicative extroverted side because that's where my comfort lies more stably. I have learned as a rising entrepreneur, you have to network as much as possible and to be successful you have to break out of that introverted shell more times than you would probably like. I've legit forced myself into a communicative state in times that were crucial to my growth, which can be very exhausting and even nerve racking at times but it a necessary evil that must be indulged in. If you identify as an introvert and can relate to any of what was just said, do not let society try to lean you towards becoming something you are not. For a long time, I felt since I was able to transition into a communicative and talkative state so easily I thought I should fully indulge in that side, society let me to believe only the talkative prosper. That false reality made me uncomfortable and I chose to walk through life in a way that made me comfortable, societies standards for my life were thrown in the trash. Embrace and appreciate that side of you and whoever accepts that part of you or not will come and go as they should.

31- JEFF

31-JEFF

ACTUAL DEFINITION (ACCORDING TO URBAN DICTIONARY) - JEFF IS A STATE OF BEING. NOT JUST A NAME; A STATE OF EXISTENCE HIGHER THAN NIRVANA

MY DEFINITION - CURSED BY DEPRESSION AND ANXIETY INTROVERTED OVER-THINKER, NEGATIVE THINKER, PASSIONATE, AMBITIOUS, INSECURE, HURT, CONFIDENT, AFRAID, SAD, CREATIVE, OWN WORST ENEMY, ATTENTIVE, COMPASSIONATE, LOVING, INQUISITIVE, NECESSARY

I had a bit of hesitation when writing out both the good and bad definitions of who I am. I do not get reminded enough (or maybe I do not acknowledge enough) the good things I have written about myself too often. Maybe my perception of my reality paired with the negative things I say about myself feel more prevalent in my life, so that is why I led with the bad and ended with the good. I have days where the negative is present for days on end and then I have days where the positivity is in full effect, but the point of this book is to put both of the good and (things that I deem) bad about myself on the forefront and face them head on in order for me to obtain a healed mental state as well get myself to accept all aspects of who I am. My mission is to learn to live with the "negative" aspects of who I am side by side rather have them on top of me weighing me down. I no longer desire to have my negativity guide me through life. Being that this is my first book that I have ever written, I felt the need to lead with transparency and express to all who indulge- with no fear how I see myself at times and show that I am aware of the consequences of having any dark thoughts/loss of love for yourself. The purpose of this book is to have you be inspired to do the same. The mission is to have you break down every word you use when describing yourself and to get to the root of why you think and feel that way about yourself and move forward with those feelings and not against them. Whether you are writing your own personal dictionary or not I want you to face yourself with no fear. This could be considered a motivational or self-help book but if I am being honest this book for me, it initially was strictly written and meant for my healing purposes and mine only. The thoughts of an audience of people to help/inspire only came after I finished. I did not come into this with others at the forefront of my mind. I desperately needed to change who I was, and I needed to self-reflect in a healthy fashion. The only way I felt I could do that was to write this book, The Avenue. This book was the healthiest avenue to peace and understanding of who I am. My only hope is that you use me as an example of what to (and not to) be like when taking the next step towards the next version of who you want to be. I honestly don't know which section of the bookstore or which genre this book will truly end up in, but I hope you are able to receive my intention and accept my thoughts without judgement. Please apply my words into your own lives (or even someone else's life), so we can all collectively heal. This is the clearest interpretation I can give you about who I am at this present time. The journey of self-discovery is truly never-ending. No matter how many books you write about yourself, or how many conversations you have with other people about who you are, it never truly ends. Knowing who you are and being comfortable with what you learn about yourself should be the true end goal in life. Perhaps after further experiences and time spent being me the next time, I write about myself again the chapter will be a lot longer, but for now this who I am, and I hope whoever comes across me or who is in my life currently will accept and appreciate me amongst all the "negative" aspects about me.

32-JOB

ACTUAL DEFINITION - A PAID POSITION OF REGULAR EMPLOYMENT

A TASK OR PIECE OF WORK, ESPECIALLY ONE THAT IS PAID

MY DEFINITION – A NECESSARY BURDEN

I have hated every job I have ever had. Since my very first job, which I believe was at a "Toys R Us" in the video game section around age 16, I truly did want to work for anyone but myself since I was younger. I never wanted to do anything that would require so much of my time that I would not be able to have an adequate amount of time for myself. My disdain for having a job was not synonymous with my work ethic, I genuinely enjoy working on things, but only things I am passionate about. The issue is from age 16 to around age 25-26, I did not have anything in my life that could keep my attention long enough, and I also didn't have anything I was truly passionate about till I got the idea to write this book and start a podcast. (Introverted Intuition available on all audio and video platforms NOW) The idea to start a podcast and write this book both became solidified possibilities around the same point in my life if you can believe it.

As this is being written out, I still have a job that pays me well enough to be able to fund the podcast and also it allowed me to fund what you're reading currently. While I will admit I am unhappy, the security to have to a stable income and benefits does really make it all worthwhile. For now. A job requires you to be on time, stay consistent, working on your tasks for 8 hours, take minimal bathroom breaks, clock in and out for lunch on time, request when you want to take a vacation, not call outs EVER even during a snowstorm (yes, my job makes you drive in blizzards) and all of that for what? $15-$17 an hour? NOT WORTH IT IN MY EYES. If I didn't have the craving to pursue entrepreneurship, I would hands down be the most miserable individual in the world. This chapter is not meant to shit on people who enjoy being stuck in the cycle of working 9-5 Monday through Friday and having a boss. If what you do for a living genuinely makes you happy, then by all means stick to it but based off my experiences of going from job to job for 10+ years, the routine has to be broken at some point. You can be paid to be yourself. You can be paid for your interests. Research and execute. I've made money off my entrepreneurial interests, but it's never been consistent but acquiring even one dollar to be me while doing what I love was more than enough for me to commit to this path so that's why I keep going because I KNOW it's possible to make a living off your interests.

This chapter is dedicated to the creatives/entrepreneurs who are like me who were sitting at the table in the break room on their lunch one day who looked out the window and have had the thought "I've got to get the fuck out of here" and decided to pour all their energy into a path of creativity and independence. It took me so long to find the confidence to pursue this path, stability versus passion was the battle that occurred in my mind for so long. I am glad passion won in the 10th round. I call a job a necessary burden because the income and health benefits that a job provides are beyond valuable, they are what gives you an opportunity to literally live as well as have the opportunity to pursue your goals in a more stable manner. A necessary experience but the burden of having to show up when someone else demands is exhausting. Having a job that will only pay when you clock in is a true burden in my eyes. No freedom involved. Living check to check is the most frustrating life to live. I've been there, I am there, and I do not and WILL NOT live this life forever. A job is a burden for creatives because after an 8-10-hour shift there's less time in the day to create. Having your energy spent at a job you do not love drains you. That energy spent could have in turn been spent towards something you enjoy. Having this divide between choosing what's best for you and what makes you happy is a frustrating crossroads to be at. The true entrepreneurs will keep going no matter how many hours they worked

prior but it's still a draining burden that exists that would not be so bad

if we got paid to do what we love when want or is our jobs paid us

wages that were reasonable. Your job will always take priority over

the passion and simultaneously keeps that passion alive so if you can,

maintain that balance until the weight shifts in a direction towards a

life where you dictate your schedule, your vacation days, and when

your pay day is.

33-KAKORRHAPHIOPHOBIA

33-KAKORRHAPHIOPHOBIA

ACTUAL DEFINITION - IS AN ABNORMAL, PERSISTENT, IRRATIONAL FEAR OF FAILURE IN CLINICAL CASES, IT'S DEBILITATING: THE FEAR OF EVEN THE MOST SUBTLE FAILURE OR DEFEAT IS SO INTENSE THAT IT RESTRICTS A PERSON FROM DOING ANYTHING AT ALL

MY DEFINITION - MY LIFE! MY ENTIRE EXISTENCE. MY BIGGEST FEAR

YES, THIS IS AN ACTUAL WORD AND YES I DON'T KNOW HOW TO PRONOUNCE IT AND I WILL BET ANY AMOUNT OF MONEY YOU CAN'T EITHIER. To be honest, I can't recall where or how I found out about this word but when I googled the definition, I was surprised to find out this is the scientific term for a feeling I couldn't properly articulate for years on end, but finally I have one. Kakorrhaphiophobia. Even reading it in my head, I still cannot pronounce it correctly. Anyways, the fear of failure is not something specific to only me. I believe this feeling is extremely common amongst the human race, specifically for the entrepreneurs/creatives. Keeping the lens focused on me for a second, the fear does manifest in everything I attempt in life. I genuinely do NOT want to fail. Ever. I do not want to let myself down. I do not want to let others down. I do not want to be an embarrassment. I do not like losing. I do not enjoy having things not go my way. These are thoughts that circle around my head whenever I embark on a new task that I am passionate about. These thoughts sometimes benefit me and boost the amount of motivation/confidence I have to accomplish whatever goals I have, but sometimes it causes me to back out of what I am working towards because the fear settles in and the thought to not try at all with the goal to avoid the pain that comes with failure becomes more appealing. "If I don't try then they'll be no pain" - something that I consistently repeated to myself. I used to say this to give myself an excuse for not trying and to put my mind at ease and to relieve myself of any potential guilt. Fooling myself basically. No matter what I am working towards, even if I am doing something as simple as cleaning my room within certain amount of time, the anxiety builds, and I fear not being able to complete even such a simple task in the time I allotted myself. It drives me nuts. I wonder if there is a cure for this because I have yet to find one. Even accomplishing goals still is not a remedy for this phobia. Eliminating expectations could be a good start but I am not entirely sure if it will work consistently. Taking away expectations would take away the self-induced pressure but not having an end goal in mind might build more anxiety. I always felt anxiety is the result what we fear could happen and depression is the result of what did happen

The yin and yang of life is pre-determined and truthfully if everything went our way 365 24/7 the world would become a bit more boring - and even knowing this, the fear is still present. What do I do about this? Is there anything that really can be done? Am I cursed with this fear for the rest of my life? I think so if I am being honest. The fact of my life is that I have experienced more failures than victories, and I believe a mild form of PTSD was developed, and I think I am cursed with this phobia for life but all I can do - all we all can do is move forward faster than the fear does. The mind will continue to convince me of a fact that is really fiction. My mind has me convinced I was cursed and conceived to fail, the disconnect between my mind and spirit must be repaired to truly stop the acknowledgment of this phobia. I will move forward as soon as I can, and I will think so positively that my mind will have no choice but to return to a state where I once again had no idea what Kakorrhaphiophobia meant.

34-LEGACY

ACTUAL DEFINITION - AN AMOUNT OF MONEY OR PROPERTY LEFT TO SOMEONE IN A WILL

MY DEFINITION - NOT JUST THE AMOUNT OF MONEY OR PROPERTY I PLAN TO LEAVE BEHIND, MY WORK, MY IMPACT, MY ART, MY ENERGY WILL BE LEFT BEHIND AND NEVER FORGOTTEN

My legacy will be solidified when I am gone. I do not think about the end of my life really ever, mostly because I don't want my thoughts to trap me there and bring about my end sooner than I want it to. But when I do end up in that space in my head, my legacy is always at the forefront of those thoughts. I want every piece of art that I create to never be forgotten; I want all the good memories I have had with people that I have encountered to be never forgotten; I want the impact my energy has contributed to the ecosystem to never be forgotten. How do I do that? How do I solidify myself into people's hearts and minds until the end of time?

Certain names come to mind that I know will never be forgotten, like Prince or Toni Morrison. In my opinion, they solidified their legacies by doing what they did in their respective fields without having their legacy on their mind at all. What I have set out to accomplish does not come close at all to comparing to what those two - and the many other individuals that fill up our history textbooks - have done, but I do know if I continue on the path, I am on then an unforgettable legacy is in my future. Although the amount of people who will never forget what I did might not compare to the amount the more well-known figures brought in, the amount I do garner will be enough for me. If at least one person does not forget then my soul will rest easy. Money and property being left behind is something I would feel stronger about wanting if I had children and if I did, I think my thoughts on the word legacy would be completely different because my children would be my legacy. The preservation of their existence would be my ultimate goal, the chances of my legacy being maintained would be guaranteed. The one thing I have learned as I have gotten older and wiser is to detach myself from the destination while embarking on this journey, we call life. Anything I could possibly want for myself at the end will be mine. I just have to isolate my vision on it, maintain faith, and get up every single day ready and willing to do the best I can and eventually everything I want will be all mine. You will garner the everlasting love and attention throughout the process because what you do is undeniable, and if you never think about the end when it is all said and done, what you have done up till that point will never be forgotten by somebody. Another message being said to myself while simultaneously speaking to you reader. Legacies are created through hard work, dedication and focus on everything but the legacy itself and since you reading this is proof that mine has been solidified and the chances that will not be forgotten by you are pretty high if you made it this far in the book. Keep reading, you'll see.

35-LOVE

ACTUAL DEFINITION - AN INTENSE FEELING OF DEEP AFFECTION

A GREAT INTEREST AND PLEASURE IN SOMETHING

FEEL A DEEP ROMANTIC OR SEXUAL ATTACHMENT TO (SOMEONE)

MY DEFINITION - INTENSE, CONFUSING, BEAUTIFUL, UNFAMILIAR, RARE, OBTAINIBLE

Love is so interesting to me. It is something we all wish to obtain whether it is love from others (friends, partners, family) or love for ourselves- all which I believe to be very difficult to obtain and maintain if you are not right within. One of the "actual" definitions of love is "an intense feeling of deep affection" and I feel this the most common form of love that people tend to fall into. Connecting physically with someone and increasing the level of affection/connection you have with someone paired with mental/emotional support ultimately adds the title of love you have with someone. Admittedly, this is the form of love I have experienced myself a few times in the past and it was truly the most magical feeling I have ever experienced. Having someone accept you for who you are while simultaneously providing you with the physical, emotional, and mental stimulation is a feeling that compares to no other. The next form of love that I believe is also common is love from one's family. The family that raised you and molded you into the individual you are today, that will support you in a way nobody else will is a form of love that unfortunately some do not get to experience. In my case, it is a feeling that I learned I do not appreciate fully while I currently still have it, but I am working through that self-created barrier with the goal of accepting this opportunity fully one day. Lastly the form of love that (I am still figuring out) is rare in my opinion is love for yourself. True love for who you are. Most people maneuver through life with acceptance of their behavior/self but do not necessarily express the love they have for themselves. Let me take the scope off of other people I do not know and focus on myself for a bit. The amount of love I have for myself has slowly grown as I have gotten to know myself a bit more, but I am still striving towards true love for Jeff. For the majority of my life, I was very lost. I hadn't known my strengths for very long and was more familiar with my weaknesses for even longer. For a long time, I did not know what I wanted to do with my life; I did not know who I was and why I was here and in turn I developed a severe inferiority complex that defined who I was for years on end. For years on end, I equated my position in life to my worth. I thought the amount of money in my bank account was synonymous with my purpose for being here. Everything I did not have in life made me less than knowing that it was not in my possession. Not knowing what's next for you is an extremely scary feeling especially when you overthink and compare your journey to others. Love for myself was nonexistent for a long ass time but as I have gotten older and developed awareness of who I am, I have slowly learned what love for self means. I had to learn to accept who I was first, I had to come to grips with the fact that who I am is who I am meant to be and there is no way to change. Love for self and love for others are conjoined; the amount of respect and affection you give to others you naturally expect back and while increasing the strength of the bond is key, those relationships are not guaranteed to last forever (if you're in a relationship I truly hope it does) but the relationship you have with yourself is inescapable and will last forever. No matter how far you go in life, you'll always have yourself to deal with. You deal with yourself way longer than you deal with others, so you might as well get to know and appreciate yourself. Love for yourself is essential to growth and peace, so I encourage everyone (including myself) to obtain love for yourself as soon as possible. Love is a very rare thing in any form of relationship you seek, but it is obtainable if you put the work in. Show respect, be attentive, support, encourage, protect not just your partners you are intimate with, but also do the same for your family and most importantly do all those things and more for yourself. I had to learn the hard way on many occasions that to properly love all the other things in your life, I discovered all I needed to know was how to love myself properly. There was no way I could truly be the ideal partner for my previous girlfriends with no appreciation or love for myself. Like with the journey of self-discovery, the journey of self-love is an equally long road to traverse but I imagine the end of the road makes the path traveled worth it. I try to be as careful as I can to not even think negative thoughts about myself as those thoughts ultimately morph into a false reality and the lack of love becomes prevalent for even longer. I encourage anyone reading this to find the nearest mirror and thoroughly gaze at yourself and say confidently that you love yourself. Make it apart of your routine to do that at least once a day. I personally do not do this, but I incorporated the habit of making sure every night before I go to bed (after I pray) to say something good about myself. No matter what it is whether it is true or not, I try to say it a few times before attempting to sleep. I fall asleep much easier when I do and when I wake up, I feel much better than I do when I go nights where I forget/do not do it. You can incorporate my personal technique or come up with something that works best for you but whatever you decide, make sure it is done regularly. Build up love for yourself no matter what. Obtain/spread the love you deserve.

36-MARATHON

36-MARATHON

ACTUAL DEFINITION - A LONG DISTANCE RUNNING RACE, STRICTLY ONE OF 26 MILES 385 YEARDS (42.195 km)

A LONG-LASTING OR DIFFICULT TASK OR OPERATION OF A SPECIFIED KIND.

MY DEFINITION - LIFE *SIGHS*

Life is exhausting as fuck. Being an ambitious, introverted individual with multiple dreams that I want manifested means I have to traverse through life with a relentless attitude. Sometimes I will have to work till I hit my limit and then conjure the energy to go past my limit. The marathon of life shows no mercy and rewards those who work hard as well as those who move with integrity. It is really on you to decide if you want to indulge on that path and what type of individual you want to be. A relentless, forward thinking, integrity filled individual or the opposite of all those things. If you have the stamina for it, you will get whatever it is you want while traversing the marathon that is life. I have personally learned that inheriting the amount of stamina needed to persevere through the difficult tasks life throws your way starts in the mind first and the body second. Being that I am actively working on my mind and body simultaneously, I am seeing results bred from the training I have done in both parts of my being. I am proving to myself that there are finish lines at the end of these marathons, but they won't ever end depending on how deep your ambitious nature is imbedded into your core. The late and GREAT Nipsey Hussle who coined the phrase, "The Marathon Continues", once said "on a mission your worst enemy is idle time" and in this marathon we call life, there is no room for any wasted time, especially if you have a clear vision when looking at what you want for yourself. Nipsey was the definition of individualism, independence, ambitious, and a hustler. Although I did not catch onto to his message/energy until it had left his body and he transitioned, everything he said in his music and interviews is still just as relevant as it was when it was first said. I recommend, to anyone who is not familiar with his music or life to close this book (with a bookmark at this spot of course) and do as much research on him as possible; and adapt bits of his beliefs and practices into your own life. The goals at the end of my personal marathon include being a successful podcast host (Introverted Intuition is the name of the show. Shameless plug). A respected and sought-after filmmaker, and popular, well-known, bestselling author (surprised?) as well as a few other things. But I would say those are the top three goals that I am chasing with everything that I am with an unwavering focus that will not dissipate until I have all of them; I will have them all. I have them all. They will be and are mine. The universe has it all planned already. It is all written out for me and I know for a fact everything I want I already have; my physical body is just playing catch up.

"A long lasting or difficult task or operation of a specified kind" is probably the most accurate "actual" definition thus far, not a single lie is told in it and the choice is yours if you want to set yourself on the track to run the marathon of life. The alternative is to literally do nothing every single day until you eventually die. It does not sound fun, so make the right choice and move forward relentlessly, break your limitations, and get what you want/deserve. Go beyond your limits as often as you can, and challenge your mind, body, and spirit to new heights; you can get past them if you believe. The Marathon Continues.

37-MONEY

37-MONEY

ACTUAL DEFINITION - A CURRENT MEDIUM OF EXCHANGE IN THE FORM OF COINS AND BANKNOTES; COINS AND BANKNOTES COLLECTIVLEY.

MY DEFINITION - A NECESSARY EVIL

My relationship with money is probably just like a lot of you reading this; I love when I have it and feel a sense of emptiness when I do not have it. No matter if you have a large or small amount, it never feels like you have enough. I remember growing up, my relationship with money was way different than it is now. It wasn't a priority but whenever I got some, it was usually for completing a chore or something and that sense of accomplishment came with five dollars. The desire to keep wanting more and more was not present until I got older, when I realized you need way more than the five dollars to literally stay alive. You are quickly taught, as soon as your view expands of the world and the bills pile up, that money is a necessity to maintain some form of peace. The flaw in this this perspective is that you will find yourself working hours upon hours slaving away for a check that is way less than you deserve to pay those piled up bills; rinse and repeat until you crack the code to financial freedom. It is a sad life. I will admit I am currently trapped in the cycle of working 80+ hours, getting paid two weeks later and repeat. It feels like hell. Truly. Like I mentioned in the, "WANT" OR "NEED" chapters, I am a bit of compulsive spender at times and I have a hard time balancing spending my money on what is going to keep me stable for the following month like bills, rent, and keeping a cap on the amount I spend on frivolous items like clothes and sneakers. The scales of balancing my funds usually tips to the side of buying what I want rather than what I need which usually ends up with me feeling guilty. The guilt paired with less dollars that was needed for a bill conjures a very dark energy in my mind. The feeling of having any amount of money that you earned to then use it how you want is such a fulfilling feeling until you hit "checkout". It feels so good to enjoy the fruits of your labor but unfortunately in my irresponsible case, I never had enough to enjoy life the way I want. All I do is try to maintain my bill schedule and make sure they are paid on time. There are practices I have adapted to my lifestyle to slowly be better with my finances, but it has been a slow burn. I have always been better at spending then saving and my high appreciation for the things in life that don't really matter (clothes, shoes, etc.) takes control and before you know it, I have an over- drafted account for the third time in the same year. It is a bad habit that I have chipped away at but have not completely broken. This is not an excuse for my behavior, but I was never taught how to be financially literate. From home to school, I was never taught how to properly budget, so I have really been freestyling the process and have been actively trying to find my way before it gets too bad. Money provides access, peace, stress, and happiness all at once and I tend to only let the negative side effects of money control my life. I would not say I am obsessed with it but it's always in the back of mind and I do desire a lot of it. Not just for me but having a lot of money could save so many lives that are directly connected to my life as well as the ones outside of it who I could help with a lot of money.

Some members of society will tell you money is not everything or that money is the root of all evil and I agree to a certain degree; it just depends on what you're willing to do with/for that money before and after you get it. My desire for money is not strong enough to cause me to compromise my integrity or relationships with anyone. I personally would be more willing to take the option of figuring out what my life will be like without it rather than potentially hurting someone or myself for it.

Money provides a double-edged sword to all our lives, but it is on you to decide what you want to do with it/what you are willing to do to get it. Coming from an irresponsible compulsive spender who buys things to fill a void, it is hard to resist the temptation but if you can, put as much as you can in your savings and pay your bills. Overdraft accounts are not pretty sights. Trust me. Being that I am so familiar with what an overdraft account looks like, I may not be the best person to listen to when it comes to money. But if anything, I have provided you with a real-life horror story that comes with using all your money responsibly. You are welcome.

38-MOTHER

38-MOTHER

ACTUAL DEFINTION - A WOMAN IN RELATION TO HER CHILD OR CHILDREN

MY DEFINITION - A PROTECTOR, A BEACON OF STRENGTH, SOMETIMES A STRANGER

I have a mother; I have had one for 28 years now, but I feel like I do not really know her at times. I can be blamed for this; my introverted nature affected even my relationships with my family members, but I feel this situation goes a bit deeper for me. Like I mentioned in the "FATHER" chapter, he abandoned my mother while she was pregnant with me and I always felt like my existence was the reason for their split. In the 90s for a young couple, I can only imagine how expensive the cost of living was WITHOUT a child, so with one it was probably even worse. Being that they were so young, I am sure they were ambitious and goal oriented (there is no way I am this way if they weren't); they had to have had things they wanted to get done and a baby definitely throws a wrench into those plans, or at the very least they halt them temporarily. I felt like I was the reason for the depression/anxiety she developed, the consistent tiredness from her having to work so much, her weight gain then weight loss; I felt responsible for it all and I felt it I did not exist none of that would. I cannot confirm any of this, but it is all what my brain had conjured and stayed in my mind since I was a youth. When I was first born, I felt that is when the disconnection in the relationship between my mother and I first started. I am aware how crazy this may sound but this was very real in my mind. This next thought might be even crazier to you. I was born prematurely, so early in fact that when I was born, my mom got sick and I was too small to be taken home. So for the first 6 months of being in this world, I was in the hospital in order to gain enough weight and to be considered healthy enough to go home. Not being in the embrace of my mother for 6 whole months or being in an unfamiliar world was not easy for me to accept, especially after being attached to her for 9 months. I am sure I was afraid and confused - although I have no memory of any of this. After talking to my therapist and a few friends about this, it makes a bit of sense that subconsciously the resentment and disconnected energy started way back then. Again, this could be a stretch, but you never know. When I was eventually brought home and grew up, like I mentioned before, taking care of a baby is expensive, especially when your family is the furthest thing from wealthy. So my mom - like everyone else in my family - had to work a lot, and that is what she did for years on end to provide a life for me; selflessly slaving away to make sure I was good at the expense of her wellbeing. Looking back, I should have appreciated this way more, but I was so selfish. She worked a lot and the majority of the little things - like making dinner and helping with homework - fell upon my grandmother's shoulders. I feel that is the second place where the disconnect manifested, which also turned into another form of subconscious resentment as well. Even amongst those moments where my grandmother was technically doing most of the providing, I never viewed her as my mother. I was able to compartmentalize the two beings for what they were and always knew who was who.

I am admitting this for the first time. I am NOT proud of this time but that resentment towards her, for a very brief period of time, was aimed towards black women as a whole. I dated some here and there early on, but there was always a lingering anger as well a lack of respect I held towards them subconsciously due to the friction of my relationship with my mother. A friction that I created. As I got older and did more self-analyzing, that eventually went away. Thankfully.

The resentment towards my mother no longer exists, and my appreciation as well as my understanding that she was never against me is clearer. With this, I was able to admire her strength more. Her ability to persevere through the abandonment of the man who aided in my birth, her ability to still grow as a woman while learning to be a mom for the first time; it was all recognized after this realization of my behavior. The selfish lens I looked through when viewing our relationship damaged my relationship not only with her but almost with black women as a whole; a view I am glad I adjusted. While the resentment no longer exists, the desire to connect is not fully there yet, but I am doing what I can at a pace that makes me comfortable. As I am writing this, she is still very much present in my life, but I am fine with not talking to her as often as I can. I think this mindset branches off the reality I created in my youth. The reality of knowing she had to work, and I wouldn't see her till there was downtime in her schedule. I love her and care about her wellbeing but the desire to chat and hang out just is not there and I wish it were. I do not feel any anger towards her, but it just feels awkward whenever we do have moments where we are communicating. That shyness comes into effect and it feels like I am forcing myself to get to know someone I do not know, and my defense mechanism is to not interact at all and just go about my business. Like I mention in the "TIME" chapter, I pay attention to the invisible clock we are all on. I am aware we are not here forever, and while I want to mend that relationship badly and I do not want any regrets, something just stops me. I want the relationship to be stronger without me wishing for a non-regretful life. Through therapy, I am uncovering what all this means and hopefully by the next book, I will have a healthy update for you, the reader. What I will say is if you have a healthy relationship with your mother keep it as stable as possible. DO NOT BE LIKE ME. The one who brought you into this world should be the most important person to you. MAKE SURE you value, protect, cherish, and maintain that relationship for as long as you can. You do not want potential regrets on your plate like I do. I love you mom. I do. I am trying to make this relationship of ours stronger...just at my own pace. Pray for me reader.

39-MOTIVATION

39-MOTIVATION

ACTUAL DEFINITION - THE REASON OR REASONS ONE HAS FOR ACTIG OR BEHAVING IN A PARTICULAR WAY

MY DEFINITION - EASY TO OBTAIN, HARD TO MAINTAIN...AT LEAST FOR ME

MOTIVATION. Another one of my arch enemies. Like my definition suggests, I personally can easily obtain motivation/inspiration to do things but utilizing it and maintaining it for more than a few days, even more than a few hours, is very difficult for me. I am admittedly a very lazy human being at times, and I feel that plays a very huge role in why I do not have the consistent level of motivation I seek. Every time something I am interested in pursuing appears in my mind, it sounds so appealing and I want to start immediately but I never do. I just sit idly and wait for the motivation to hit me hard enough that I start whenever that moment comes. That is something I am working on (like everything else I mentioned up till this point) but in addition to the laziness comes a hefty side of overthinking and a portion of confusion for dessert.

Absorbing inspiration to create from a YouTube video I am watching for example feels very good and I get excited to the point where I am about to begin what I was inspired to do, then my mind completely blanks. I am confused as to where to start. I was inspired by watching someone else do something and I clearly want to do my own version of what I saw but when I try to create my own version of that, my mind tells me it is very difficult to make mine just as good - if not better. Then after what I was just watching is over, I end up overthinking myself into a corner. I think about time a lot, so I try not rush things. I end up telling myself I have plenty of time and as time is passing, I then notice plenty of time flew by with no progress to show for it. I have done nothing up till that realization hits, then the guilt settles in. I usually, always plan in my head what my schedule will be for the next few days at the start of the week. If there's a proper opening where I know for a fact I am doing nothing on a specific day, I usually brush my motivation to the side and push back what I actually wanted to do to that day and I end up doing nothing. That process of conjuring motivation repeats until I EVENTUALLY get it done. This book's creative process was no different! My motivations to make this book did not maintain; my motivations come and go when they please and I feel I have no control unless I force it. My desire to write this book was not synonymous with my effort. I do not want to do anything most days out the year, but you can bet your bottom dollar I am beating myself up mentally for not doing anything at all on those days where I'm lounging. I have learned the fruits of my labor - the benefits and feelings of victory after doing what I set out to accomplish mean so much more to me and also aid in my continued motivation to keep working. But if I could give all this up to just get paid to do nothing, I really would. While the results breed motivation for me, the hardest part is getting/maintaining the motivation to get those results.

Point of this chapter? The moral of this story? Work when you can and are able to and do NOT beat yourself up when you do not do anything for a full day. It is a toxic cycle you will end up trapping yourself in and eventually the love for yourself will dissipate faster than it took for you to conjure it. Motivation comes and goes but this life of ours only comes around once (many times if you believe in reincarnation) but when you get the motivation to do something, to alter your reality a bit, do everything you can to hold onto it. Just know it is cool to be lazy like me too sometimes, in moderation. Earn your leisure.

40-MUSIC

40-MUSIC

ACTUAL DEFINITION - VOICE OR INSTRUMENTAL SOUNDS (OR BOTH) COMBINED IN SUCH A WAY AS TO PRODUCE BEAUTY OF FORM, HARMONY, AND EXPRESSION OF EMOTION

MY DEFINITION - THERAPUTIC, BENEFICIAL, NECESSARY. THE WORLD WOULD BE A LOT WORSE WITHOUT IT

I LOVE MUSIC SO MUCH. MY LOVE FOR HIP HOP, R&B, JAZZ, POP ROCK, INSTRUMENTALS, KNOWS NO BOUNDS AND I AM SO GRATEFUL FOR EVERY ARTIST THAT CREATES THESE BEAUTIFUL SOUNDS. Without music, this world would be SO much worse. It would be a lot quieter. A lot blander. Without music, the world would be a much darker place; the peace music provides knows no bounds. I know for a fact that I personally would be a lot sadder if every song ever created did not exist anymore. My relationship with music runs deep, so deep in fact it is almost as if I am in love with the music and the artists who create it. The one-way connection between the consumer and the artist is built organically, especially if the artist is consistently creating great music. Music for me is audio therapy, there is literally a song for every type of mood you could be in as well as a lyric or two that are guaranteed to be synonymous with your life in some way. Deeper than the lyrics and the artist, the sounds, the feelings they provide needs to be highlighted more. The energy these amazingly talented producers and composers create are the real treat for me musically. I always focus on the instrumentation before the lyrics; the feeling I get is the determining factor if I will like the song as a whole or not. All music producers get my respect and acknowledgement, always. The lyrics are what we hear and relate to, but the instrumentation is what makes us feel and dance. A lot of times particularly in my case, even cry. My favorite genres of music are (in no particular order because that's too hard) R&B, Hip Hop, Jazz, and Pop Rock. In addition, I love to listen to scores/soundtracks from video games and television shows as well. I feel these soundtracks do NOT get enough praise when compared to a Michael Jackson album for example but that is neither here nor there. I personally am not musically inclined enough to create my own music (yet), but I am content with that fact because there's such an extreme influx in the amount of music that is released these days, I am not mad my contribution to the musical game isn't real yet. I would rather hear the professionals make music anyways. Although you must search really hard for the music/artists with substance know, it's out there; you just have to be willing to weed through the stuff that isn't as good in order to find the stuff that's worth a listen. Narrowing down even a few of my favorite musical acts is tough but just a few to name are Prince, Erykah Badu, Jay Z, Roy Ayers, Ella Fitzgerald, Mac Quayle, HIM (band from Finland), King Krule, The Doors, Janelle Monae, and many more. Those were just few that came to mind that I definitely would recommend you check them all out! I can say with no hesitation that these artists, as well as the many that I did not name, have played a major role in my life, and have healed me with their music while also consistently providing me with audio therapy that I am forever grateful for. I could gush on and on about my love music but what I will repeat is that the world would be so much worse without music, and I am so glad that version of the world is not a reality. I am going to make a song of my own one day, whenever I can conjure and maintain the confidence in my singing voice. I have never gone a day without listening to music and I never plan to. Music is the healthiest and most consistent escape from the darkness that my depression and anxiety conjure. Music provides feelings like no other medium that exists, and I am eternally grateful for all the artists, producers, and composers who strive to make music that fuels peoples' souls. The artists that make music solely to get a few more dollars in their bank account and make substance-less music, you have my appreciation as well, although my respect level is not as high. I have many of my best ideas, as well as my most impact self-reflective moments while listening to music, so my gratefulness for music runs a bit deeper than the average consumer. Music videos also play a major role in my life as well. Although the quality of music videos has diminished and they have become more simplistic, the appreciation for the song is always heightened for me when it is paired with a visual. The visual is a complete reflection of the artists intention and thoughts when they were making the song and I appreciate having the full picture to interpret. I am eternally grateful to have the open mind that I do when it comes to music. I embrace and like a lot of different types of music and my hope is that the children that I will (hopefully) have will be the same way. Thank god for music.

41-NEED

41-NEED(S)

ACTUAL DEFINITION - REQUIRE (SOMETHING) BECAUSE IT IS ESSENTIAL OR VERY IMPORTANT. OF NECESSITY

MY DEFINITION - MORE IMPORTANT THAN THE WANTS.

In my mind, our needs are the things in our life that we literally need to be stable enough in order for us to not lose our sanity. Our bills need to be paid, our fridges need to be stocked, our cars need to be filled with gas, our girlfriends need gifts for their birthday; all things we need to stay alive. Somehow even with my acknowledgment of this fact, my "wants" tend to outweigh my "needs" and in turn have caused a lot of self-sabotage. Like I mentioned in the "MONEY" chapter, I have been completely irresponsible with my money time after time and I had to learn how to be better. It took a lot of over-drafted accounts and disappointed girlfriends for me to realize that the "needs", the important things always come first. I was never taught how to be financially literate. Some might think it is common sense to save more than you spend but for me I learned in the worst way possible. I need direct lessons in order to understand and comprehend. I was really good at a lot growing up in school, specifically writing if you haven't noticed thus far but the simple things went over my head. Creatively, I was on point, but I missed a lot of lessons that were just as necessary for my growth. I have failed and messed my way up many of times, and it all led me to understand my mistakes. I am a compulsive spender, not a great planner, and overall just really dumb at times but the bigger picture I am trying to paint is comparing the "wants" and "needs" in life you need to accept that sometimes you have to try and fail in life to get the understanding of the lessons that are thrown your way. You must fuck up repeatedly in order to grow past the bad behavior you are accustomed to. You are always going to want things out of this life but check yourself before you indulge and MAKE SURE your "needs" are in order. Do not go broke repeatedly/piss off a girlfriend like I did. Being as ambitious as I am, there are so many things I must pay for in order to get further ahead in life. The manufacturing of this book is a perfect example. I do not want to get into specifics but looking at the amounts I would have to pay for the perfect quality is ridiculous but a necessary burden. Without the necessary funds available in my accounts, I will never truly be happy. The fact is money is needed, a lot of it. Just to live, you need a healthy amount of money in your pockets, so re-reminding myself of these basic principles I strive to maintain a healthier balance between my "wants" and "needs".

42-OPINIONATED

42-OPINIONATED

ACTUAL DEFINITION - CONCEITEDLY ASSERTIVE AND DOGMATIC ONES OPINIONS

MY DEFINITION - A DOUBLE EDGED. BEING THIS WAY WILL OFFEND, HURT, AND CONFUSE PEOPLE AT TIMES BUT IT'S A BLESSING TO BE THIS WAY. EMBRACE IT AND STAND FIRM ALWAYS

Having an opinion will have people judge you. Having an opinion will have people hate you. Having an opinion will have people respect you. Whatever the outcome is after your opinion is expressed, DO NOT waver from it, and do not take it back. To those who do not accept your opinion, know they do not have to; your opinion is not always right but still express it with no fear. I have always been an opinionated individual, I found myself getting into long winded discussions about topics I was passionate about from a young age and it got me a lot of trouble especially in school and in church. Being inquisitive and opinionated comes off as being disrespectful and a smartass to adults when you are a child and at times these adults would tell me things like "that is not polite" or "you don't understand because you're not old enough" and whether they were conscious of it or not I felt as though they were trying to quiet my individuality and stop me from having the ability/confidence to stand firm on my beliefs/curious nature. Fast forward to present day, I have an opinion on most things and during certain times when I have expressed it, I have offended people to the point where they are no longer in my life (by their choice) and I feel that is for a few reasons. One reason being discomfort within themselves. I feel the resistance and anger towards someone with a firm stance on their beliefs comes from someone who is not that sure of themselves let alone what they are arguing. Confidence in a belief stems from deeper within. To the confident, the faith opinionated individuals have in themselves knows no bounds, especially it when it comes to a stance in a back forth. On the flip side, people who are the complete opposite can sense the unfamiliar energy and in turn resist it. Ultimately lashing out against what they wish they had, rather than the topic of the disagreement.

Being opinionated is truly a double-edged sword because you can either affect, inspire, and potentially change someone's view on a topic or conjure a negative energy you never asked for. Knowing that, again do not fear expressing yourself. Keeping your thoughts caged in is not a healthy experience as time goes on and you will let these moments pass by you without ever getting in on a conversation. When I was younger, specifically around the time I was in middle school going into high school era, I was still extremely deep rooted in my shyness. I would let certain opinions be said about a specific topic in class or even about me by the kids who made jokes about me just go with no response from me. I never had the confidence in my voice to retort. I did not defend myself for a very a long time. I was a literal walking mat for opinions, the synchronization between my shyness and insecurities crippled any hope of expressing myself. I am so glad I got out of that because if I did not, I would still be stepped on till this day. I will remain opinionated to the end of my days and will stand firm no matter how convincing the argument is against my opinion. Do not put your opinion out there with the intention of trying to cause conflict or even to impress anyone. Do it because you value your thoughts and want to contribute to the dialogue. REMAIN STURDY WITH YOUR OPINION ALWAYS. EXPRESS IT WITH NO FEAR. DON'T SUBSCRIBE TO GROUP THINK. But do not ever forget, although you may express your opinion with no fear in your heart know, YOUR opinion is strictly that. Your opinion can be wrong. It is not a fact and people CAN and WILL challenge it at times, so be prepared for the resistance. It is a bit ironic how this whole chapter is my opinion.

43-OVERTHINKING

43-OVERTHINKING

ACTUAL DEFINITION - THINK ABOUT (SOMETHING) TOO MUCH OR FOR TOO LONG.

MY DEFINITION - A NEVER ENDING BATTLE. HOW DO I STOP?!

Being an only child who did not have an imaginary friend to talk to; all I had were the conversations in my head to swirl around all day and night. Mixing that with an extremely introverted nature and you get the OG of overthinking, aka me your humble author. I literally do not know how to stop overthinking every decision, moment, and experience that I go through, and I wish I did but just like depression I feel this is another irremovable curse that must be accepted. Acceptance of the curse feels like the logical step towards changing and ultimately overthinking less, but I have not found a concrete way to stop. My overthinking usually consists of me thinking about every step leading up to, during and after an experience and usually what the aftermath will be weeks after the situation/experience has come and gone. It is bad. Really bad. I do not know how to stop. Most of my overthinking unfortunately consists of negative thinking and it halts a lot of my progress and simultaneously causes me to waste a lot of time. For that fact alone, I do actively attempt to keep my thoughts present but again, it's really hard to do consistently. I am my own personal roadblock. I get in my way consistently; my awareness is so high of this problem but the effort towards applying change fails in comparison. Overthinking is basically a never-ending battle for control of my spirit between my mind, heart, and my physical being is caught in the middle of it. It is funny I have always wanted siblings and being that my mind and heart live together and inhabit my being in separate forms, maybe I am the older sibling and these two are the younger siblings I always wanted fighting for control of my attention. Huh. Weird thought but the universe plays zero games at all, that thought is not accident, I know that for sure. Even when I am venting and receiving words of affirmation, I am overthinking the true intention of the person sending that energy my way. Also, when I need an ear to vent to, I think about how I'm making who I am venting to feel deep down. I overly think about what they will think of me once I am done spilling my guts and when we separate, I wonder what's on their mind when they have time to fully adjust to everything I just put on their shoulders. A paralyzing feeling. Overthinking stops me from venting at times because I never want to be a bother. Overthinking has stopped me from pursing a girl I like, going to a party, applying for a job. So much has NOT been done because I overthink, but I still have managed to press forward in life despite the anchor I have attached myself to. Throughout this self-reflective journey I have been on, I faced the truth that there is a severe disconnect between my mind, body, and spirit and if this relationship does not improve, I will be forever doomed to an overthought, unhappy life. My mind and the little negative voices that linger inside have guided the other two parts of me for the majority of my life and have halted so many great opportunities for me. No longer will I allow that to happen. I strive to trust my gut feeling more and not allow the negative voices in my head to control the trajectory of my journey. No longer will I overthink.

44-PEACE

44-PEACE

**ACTUAL DEFINITION - FREEDOM FROM DISTURBANCE;
TRANQUILITY**

**MY DEFINITION-The ULTIMATE GOAL IN LIFE. WHAT WE ALL
WANT AND WHAT MOST OF US DESERVE**

Peace is a concept that can be interpreted in many ways, but I feel collectively we are all working towards them all in some way. Peace of mind. Peace in our own individual universes. World Peace. The "actual" definition of peace is very interesting to me and as I researched it, I wrote out a bunch of thoughts (that you are about to read) that flooded my mind. "Freedom from disturbance". For an introverted over-thinker like myself, freedom from disturbance seems like such an otherworldly concept, but deep down, I want it to be true so damn bad. As an over-thinker, disturbance is what I am plagued by consistently no matter what the first thought is. It is a struggle to quiet the storm and like they say, "your thoughts become things", those "things" are bits of my reality I shape that ultimately end up causing peace to be further and further away from me. Like my definition says, peace is the ultimate goal in life; that's what I want for my life more than anything else. The peace I desire is mixture of tangible objects that provide security and comfort for myself, family, and friends i.e.: money (a lot of it) an amount so high that it provides an everlasting amount of freedom from disturbance, the freedom to allow my family to do whatever they desire no matter what that is. An intangible form of peace that I desire comes in the form of stillness and silence within.

All I want is for me to go days, months, and years without a harmful/negative thought floating within my subconscious, and while it is my choice to indulge in that darkness, I want the option of acknowledgement of that negativity to be gone. I feel if I have all the tangible desires in check, the intangible would follow suit right behind it and thus peace would be achieved for me. Money is not everything, but you need it to do everything. I do not create with money on the forefront of my mind but it's always lingering in the background and I know a hefty amount is what I need and deserve, it's what my family deserves to live how they want rather than them wishing and praying they were. More tangible forms of peace include a family of my own. Having a unit of my own that I created would also free me from any disturbances and create intangible moments (memories) that will be irreplaceable and be more valuable than anything I could possibly imagine obtaining. As my overthinking, negative mind would have it though, the thought of money lingers in my mind even when imagining the concept of having a family. To be able to efficiently and consistently protect and provide for you family, you need money. A lot of it. As ambitious as I am, I know I will crack the code to financial freedom. One day soon.

So how do you acquire peace? Coming from me, the overthinking introvert, I do not know the exact step by step process to obtain everything I desire but what I do know is it won't just fall in my lap. If it somehow does, you can best believe I will be holding on TIGHT. In all seriousness, find something to do consistently that does not cause your head to spin but rather make your heart feel full and peace should follow suit. That alone could be defined as peace, doing what you love regularly whether you are making money from it or not; that seems like true peace. For me I have found things that provide room for me to relax and not let anything on the perimeter of my life inside and invade my happiness. Although those things do not provide me with the funds necessary to change my life and the lives of the ones I love, I know they will one day if I keep at it. Try and fail at everything till you find that one thing you cannot help but to go back to everyday. Peace is obtainable. Trust.

45-PERSEVERANCE

**ACTUAL DEFINITION- PERSISTANCE IN DOING
SOMETHING DESPITE DIFFICULTY OR DELAY IN
ACHIEVING SUCCESS**

MY DEFINITION- A NECESSARY INGRIDIENT TO VICTORY

With all that I have been through in life, whether it be from the
problems the universe put in my path or the problems I put in my own
way, I somehow have managed to persevere through it all and live to
write about it. The ability to be able to persevere no matter what

happens is an interesting skill to have. I feel it is something you can either be born with and have naturally or it is a skill that is taught through experiencing wins and losses. Let me explain. Everyone is born with a specific type of DNA, how that it is utilized is largely based upon how you were raised. So naturally, if the ones who are raising you have a go getter, never stop moving forward, ambitious attitude, there is a good, but not guaranteed, chance the ability to persevere will be embedded in you before you know how to do long division. It may not manifest immediately but I am SURE the parents with that attitude would strive to implant it into your brain early on. On the flip side of the perseverance coin, I think you can grow into having the ability to persevere through every situation. I believe this is the version of perseverance I personally gained. Whether you are self-inducing yourself with losses and stress, depending on who you are, something will click in your mind and you will get sick on the pain/stress that comes with failure. I have experienced too much of that, the discomforting feeling that came with those losses became too much to bare and the desire for change became equally unbearable to carry. So I had to transmute that desire into actual work to manifest the changes I wanted. Even with the self-induced depressive states and extreme laziness, I managed to fight through it all and I somehow accomplished what I set out to achieve many times in life. Even when my depression was at its peak and I was committed to the idea of killing myself, somehow, I fought through and persevered and eventually manifested this book you are reading. The skill to persevere is either in you, or it is not. Failure is still a prevalent medium on the path of progression but as you experience it more, you learn how to move around it and adjust to the times that you cannot avoid it. The ability to persevere is dependent on you, how much you desire change in life, and how you react to the failures that come your way all falls on the strength of your will. Having been on both sides of the spectrum, on the side of wanting to give up versus persevering past that thought I have full awareness of what both feelings are like. If an overthinking, insecure, ambitious individual can move forward, you can too. Tap into that strength; accept the fact that you will not always win and keep moving forward. At times I have questioned why I have this ability. I have been at my lowest on many occasions but here I remain, and I seriously wonder why. At times I have thought my ancestors' blood that flows through me activates and causes me to keep going. Other times I thought it is my subconscious; my true self keeping me afloat. Whatever it is, I am grateful to be blessed with ability to persevere through it all. If I ever got the opportunity to talk with him, I would tell my younger self to embrace the strength you have. You may not see it right away, you may not experience it consistently, but just know it exists and when you are able to tap into it, you will be invincible. Persevere through the madness in your mind, and the reality that mind creates. Keep going.

46-PRESSURE

ACTUAL DEFINITION - CONTINUOUS PHYSICAL FORCE EXERTED ON OR AGANINST AN OBJECT BY SOMETHING IN CONTACT WITH IT.

THE USE OF PERSUASION, INFLUENCE, OR INTIMIDATION TO MAKE SOMEONE OR SOMETHING

The weight of the expectations we have for ourselves adds an unbearable amount of pressure to our shoulders. As you can guess, an overthinking, pessimistic individual like myself is all too familiar with the feeling of that weight. My pessimistic attitude aside, deep down in the depths of my core, I do believe in myself and do know everything I want out of this life I will have one day. However, since I believe in myself so highly, I end up adding pressure on myself to do everything I can to make these dreams come true at a pace that just isn't possible right away - in turn, cultivating doubt and disappointment that I create for myself. The only solution that I have found for myself to relieve the pressure from my shoulders is to keep believing, to work hard enough to the point where the beliefs are proven correct and the results of my hard work are tangible. That is personally what works for me, but if I could give any advice to anyone who does the same, someone who finds themselves in self-induced pressure filled scenarios consistently, I would remind them these situations do not necessarily mean you have bad luck and are not strong enough to handle yourself under pressure; it just means you aren't fully aware of the cycle you are caught in. As I kept putting myself into more pressure filled scenarios, I began to acknowledge the pressure itself. I realized it was manifested from my own mind. So if I took that power away from myself, I would maneuver through any situation I am in the middle of pressure free and confidently only. I would recommend you put as much belief into the positive thoughts as much as you do into the negative ones. Coming from me, the overthinking pessimistic individual, that advice probably does not hold much weight, but this is a reminder for me as well; so let us strive to change together. It is way easier said than done but it feels possible. The reality you create all starts up top (*points to head*) and will be shaped by however you think; it will be in that very same head of yours. If the thoughts are all focused, controlled, and positive, the pressure will dissipate sooner than it appeared.

Pressure and confidence are synonymous with each other. For example, I have done public speaking events in the past and till this day, I typically get the feeling of nervousness before every podcast recording. Even knowing that I am 100+ episodes deep, the thought of leaving myself open to be judged and knowing I am being watched/heard is nerve racking. These thoughts breed the lack of confidence regardless of how many times I have done it. Thus allowing the pressure to enter the fray. Even knowing that I have done it many times and made it through successfully, the pressure to repeat the successful moments builds and it becomes a very nerve-racking experience leading up to the moment of truth, the time to record. Usually in those moments when the pressure is present in that same moment, I am doing everything I can to remain present and record a podcast without acknowledgement of my past experiences as well as the results to come from that present moment. What I do to also relieve pressure - and this might sound a bit crazy - but I literally convince myself before any situation I am in that my life depends on my success' and I convince myself that there is no going back so I need to do the best I can or else. I force my mental state into a belief that I have no choice but to succeed. Super extreme I know, but it works most of the time. Pressure is not real. The weight is manifested from your own brain and if you have the mental toughness to convince yourself that the weight is not real, and you will win every time. Or you can just be like me and think your life is dependent on your success and see how that works. Your choice. No pressure though.

47-PURPOSE

ACTUAL DEFINITION - THE REASON FOR WHICH SOMETHING IS DONE OR CREATED OR FOR WHICH SOMETHING EXISTS.

MY DEFINITION - FIND YOURS

Why am I here? Why was I born?? In the grand scheme of the progression of time, does my existence mean much and will anything I am doing be worth it in the end??? A few questions I have asked myself during certain points of my life and till this day I do not have the answers to any of those questions, but I do know I am meant to be here. Throughout much of my youth, I felt as if I was a waste of flesh who was just taking up room on the planet. A harsh way of thinking, but when you are stuck in the cycle of working and going home to do nothing; then rinsing and repeating this cycle, it's very hard to think differently. I felt that way until I found things that I truly love doing and I honestly believe that is one secret to discovering your purpose. Finding what makes your heart sing and your cheeks hurt from smiling too hard whenever you are doing it is the first step to figuring out why you are here. Whatever it is that you decide to indulge in can manifest a purpose, something simple can breed a joy filled life, where you are doing what you love consistently. That in turn can produce a domino effect of inspiration and what you do can end up being the spark to change someone else's life. WHO KNOWS- the possibilities are endless; you just have try shit until one thing sticks. For me, my interests are very vast, and I liked doing a lot of things but couldn't stick to one thing for very long due to my lack of belief in myself, but I never gave up searching for my purpose and now a manifested extension of my purpose is in your hands currently. I am here to heal the world. Whether it is through tangible mediums like this book or an intangible form like the energy I emit, I am here to help those who need it. Both good and bad explanations can be given as to why we all exist but which category you go under is all dependent on your personal belief in your existence as well as your willingness to find your reasoning for being here. You are here for whatever reason you want to be. If you want to stay inside and eat chocolate ice cream for the rest of your life, then you can and that can be your legacy. Although I DO NOT recommend that life (outside of rainy days with no plans), I encourage anyone who is maneuvering through this life to not follow my path fully. Do not tell yourself that you are not meant to be here because you really are. I wish I had this mentality way sooner. I would have saved myself many tears when I was questioning why I was here. We all have an opportunity to shape the world in a good or bad way but the beautiful about thing life is you have the ability to choose which path you decide to take for yourself.

So to discover your purpose, all you must do is choose to find it and the universe will provide the rest. I had to traverse through the darkest corners of my mind to even say anything like all this and although I am DEFINETLY no expert on life, I do know all I had to do was look within and live my life how I wanted rather than give up in order to gain this mentality. Purpose your purpose with no fear. You are meant to be here. Please do not give up; your purpose will reveal itself eventually. You just have to be focused enough to discover its location.

48-RELAX

48-RELAX

ACTUAL DEFINITION- MAKE OR BECOME LESS TENSE OR ANXIOUS

MAKE (A RULE OR RESTRICTION) LESS STRICT WHILE NOT ABOLISHING IT.

MY DEFINITION - A NECESSARY/HARD THING TO DO AT TIMES. BREEDS COMPLACENCY.

Relax huh? How do you do that when there is so much to do? How do you relax when your mind is always running? How do you relax when your ambition consumes your reality and all you are thinking about is how to manifest your goals??? I have yet to answer any of these questions because my mind is so loud, the idea of relaxing for an extended period of time is drowned out by the loud reminders from my mind that I am not here forever and that there's no time to relax. I feel like so much time has been wasted thus far and I need to keep going before my time is up. Do not get me wrong, I can be an extremely lazy individual at times; I do not mind being still but for more than a few hours to a day feels like such a waste. I think for me, once I discovered things I am truly passionate about I adopted the thought process of never wanting to take a break again. I didn't want to go back to a point in my reality where I was living like I didn't have a passion; I didn't want much free time ever. I wanted to earn my leisure rather than take it every chance I got. I took my passions and decided to run with them for as long as I could without ever looking back, and I am aware that's an admirable mindset to have but I am also aware how important relaxing, and resetting is. It is just hard to stop once you have started. Taking the time to relax, reflect, and reset honestly will probably help an ambitious individual like myself ascend even further ahead, but I cannot shake the acknowledgment of time. Time is the only constant. We are not here forever so taking an extended period of time to relax, let alone a single day feels like a waste of the precious time we have left. I am actively trying to be patient with my life and do try to not exhaust myself.

Both my definition and the actual definition of the word "RELAX" are two things I will have to re-read many times in order to truly understand the concept. I am sure my fellow entrepreneurs, creatives, workers etc. can relate to me on some level, but in order for us to keep doing whatever it is we are doing, we have to relax at some point during the journey. However, we should not relax for too long on our way towards our destination. The idea of relaxing when there is so much to accomplish is almost terrifying to think about. Missing a day when you could be ahead two days sounds way better in my mind. Getting something done today so tomorrow is not as exhausting sounds great ideally but I would rather keep going every day regardless of how exhausted I feel. Relaxing seems so hard. Know what? I am going to end this chapter here and if you did not start your day/night with this chapter, you will practice the concept of relaxing as well. Even if reading this is a medium to relaxation for you, close this book up for the day/night and relax then come back tomorrow with a clear head and refreshed mind and body. See you in the next chapter!

49-SELFISH

49-SELFISH

ACTUAL DEFINITION - (OF A PERSON, ACTION,OR MOTIVE) LACKING CONSIDERATION FOR OTHERS; CONCERNED CHIEFLY WITH ONES OWN PERSONAL PROFIT OR PLEASURE

MY DEFINITION - A TOXIC BUT SOMETIMES NECESSARY TRAIT

Having a selfish attitude is something we all have deep down but most of us do not choose to own it due to whatever reason we use as an excuse (society, insecurity who knows). For me personally, I choose to claim mine with no hesitation. First, I want to begin with the perception of being selfish that people are against (which is warranted) and then I will present my experience with being selfish and how it is has benefited me in certain moments of my life. Like the "actual" definition of the word SELFISH states "lacking consideration for others" is truly a negative aspect of selfishness which can breed situations where someone would rather turn a blind eye to an injustice without any hesitation, as opposed to selflessly helping and diffusing a potentially fatal encounter. Too many have so many other things to worry about and would rather not compromise their own situation to help someone else; I understand but I do not respect it. Those who are selfish are also very greedy individuals who take and take without any concern that they will be affecting lives; I believe the pharmaceutical industry is a prime example of this. These medications have hundreds of thousand-dollar price tags and without the proper form of insurance, a sickly individual could lose their life over a price they can't afford that is controlled by some bigwig in an office with a nice suit who only cares about their next deposit. America, huh? The negative aspects of a selfish individual can go on and on, but the immediate perception society paints is that selfish individuals think about, only support, and aim to uplift themselves in a negative way. If what I said earlier wasn't proof of that, then I do not know what is. When the word selfish is brought up in association with someone, it is immediately set to a negative connotation on a person's character, but in my experiences in the brief times I have been selfish, it has done nothing but benefit me. I hope in the process I did not end up hurting anyone but the intention with my selfishness was solely for my own protection/peace.

One example of a time I chose to be selfish and it benefited me was back in the days of high school where I would consistently succumb to peer pressure and actively choose to smoke weed and be with my friends rather than doing my schoolwork. This was a regular occurrence, until I one day decided to fight against the self-induced peer pressure I put on myself to maintain a certain image to then

embrace my selfish side and ignore the tempting offers my friends

made. I chose to instead not answer the text messages, phone calls,

and thoughts that tried to lead me to give and go out. I chose to stay

inside and work on my homework and get my grades up. Selfish and

smart. A cliché answer but another example I have stems from a

relationship I had and although I was very much in love with this

woman, I was very content with our situation. I started to feel as

though the energy I was giving was not being reciprocated. For a

whole year, I just accepted those feelings of discomfort and I dealt

with it because I felt like a love like that couldn't be recaptured so I

stuck around and endured the halfhearted energy until one day I woke

up and decided to take control. With that my true feelings manifested,

and I ended up leaving the situation before the resentment for her

started to build. I left so I could be happy and feel like I was

appreciated somewhere else. No matter how long we had been

together and no matter how long it would take to find the feeling of

reciprocation with someone else, did not matter to me. I had to move

with selfishness and confidently accept my decision for my own peace

of mind. Ever since then, in this current time I have yet to find another

relationship like that (the highs were great, but the lows were

unbearable) and I feel so much better knowing I made a decision that

was selfishly beneficial for me without caring how it affected my partner at the time. I hope no true harm came to here from that decision, but I had to do it. Selfishness is truly a double-edged sword and depending how you emit that selfish nature, it can either expand upon or destroy your reality and relationships. Choose wisely.

50-SELFLESS

50-SELFLESS

ACTUAL DEFINITION - CONCERNED MORE WITH THE NEEDS AND WISHES OF OTHERS THAN WITH ONES OWN; UNSELFISH

MY DEFINITION- A TRAIT WE NEED MORE OF IN THE ECOSYSTEM

A selfless attitude is an attribute that the majority of humanity probably has deep down in their spirit, but they don't access it as often as they should. However, if they did collectively, I KNOW we could make this planet a better; more sustainable place to live. I don't think having a selfless attitude is something that can be taught in a classroom or anything, but I do believe it can be inherited by being shown examples of what a selfless attitude can do – and hopefully the one observing will adapt that same attitude. That is what worked for me honestly, observing my family members who are devoted to Christ, who always expressed to me the idea of blessing others without the intention of getting blessed back, but instead they said I should choose to bless others only with the intention to help and leave it at that. You will be blessed eventually, regardless if it's immediately after doing the good deed or not, the blessings will return to you in some way. Just do not seek that blessing when helping, it will come on its own time. That is probably the only practice I adapted from that time of my life when Christianity was present in my life when I think about it. I also believe selflessness (like being selfish) is a choice that can affect your life in both positive and negative ways if you are not careful. In my mind, a selfless individual is a giver, someone who would give their last to help someone in need. That is how I am at least, and in my experiences, certain individuals have taken advantage of my kindness and used me repeatedly. This happened to me on multiple occasions, that I cannot forget, I am not sure if I can even forgive. These individual's wore the mask of authenticity so well, I was none the wiser. While some would say I was naïve, I would say I was genuine, trusting, and comfortable with the idea of helping but in the end, I got the short end of the stick constantly. These situations honestly, till this day, have made me less of a trusting person, but I am still a firm believer in karma. So my selflessness has not waivered fully, but I still try my best to move as cautiously as I can. That is pretty much the only advice I can give to my fellow overly selfless individuals, move cautiously, and move without the intention of getting anything back for your good deeds. Move with the intention of helping and leave it at that. The universe will reward you in its own way on its own time, most times it will happen when you least expect it or need it the most. I am attracted to selfless people, to do something for someone other yourself or immediate family is BIG and a real testament to your character. Unfortunately, some of these non-profits work under the guise of wanting to help but when the lights turn off for the day, somebody in the backroom of the company is counting the money made and pocketing it for themself. This is an assumption, but when I have seen one too many stories about money being sent to charities that has gone missing, what else am I supposed to think? Be cautious when you decide to send your money to a "good cause". Do not be fooled, and I truly hope you do not get as scared as I am when it comes to fully trusting people, but my past experiences have left me jaded. The amount of time it has taken me to rebuild genuine trust in people after being betrayed on many of occasions has been a bit of a slow burn but with each new day and each new genuine individual I encounter, it becomes a bit easier to trust. If you are naturally a selfless person who cannot help but to aid someone in a time of need, know that you have a trait that is uniquely to you. Most don't care about anyone other than themselves, so maintain that attitude for as long as you can but just know there are ones out there who seek to control and monetize their businesses off people like you. So be careful. My grandmother is the prime example of a true naïve empathetic individual. She gives and helps every chance she gets; she has been scammed, had money stolen, and had people lie right to her face but she still gives. Her forgiving and understanding spirit are at a level I wish to achieve internally one day. Being that I am equally naïve and empathetic, my naïve mind tells me that everyone on this planet has an empathetic/selfless side within them and will use it with no hesitation or hidden motives behind those actions. I would like to think there is not a single person on this planet who is dark enough to turn a blind eye to injustice. My heart tells me that a level of selfishness isn't as real as I think it is. I know I am wrong, but my naïve mind won't let me give up hope in other people, no matter how bad I have been wronged I still believe. While I have awareness of the dark side of humanity, I know many are brave enough to act on their desire to be selfless without a hidden agenda and I will always appreciate those who do. I hope this shift occurs worldwide one day and everyone will eventually care about the wellbeing of complete strangers wholeheartedly and decide to help others whenever they can. Move cautiously, help as many as you can and be aware of everyone who enters your space because they may use your selfless nature to their advantage. Help with the desire to truly help, with no hope of getting something in return. Do not publicize your good deeds and save the world in the way that works best for you.

51-SHY

51-SHY

ACTUAL DEFINITION - BEING RESERVED OR HAVING OR SHOWING NERVOUSNESS OR TIMIDITY IN THE COMPANY OF OTHER PEOPLE

MY DEFINITION - MY MIDDLE NAME

A trait I have held with me since I was younger, and I am not sure if I will ever be able to dismiss it completely. I vividly remember many moments in my life where I have interacted with someone new and the shyness kicks in almost immediately like clockwork. My throat gets dryer, I sweat intensely, and I start to feel much heavier, thus fully transitioning me into a shy state. As I have gotten older, I have been able to find ways to maneuver out of it. But with certain individuals, specifically women I am genuinely interested in, that shy side always tends to rear its head. My introverted nature paired with my tendency to overthink, all play a part in the manifestation of the shyness. A few moments in my life the intense shyness I carried with me, specifically in high school/the early months of college, caused me to develop a strong disdain for myself. I couldn't stand being who I was, no matter what I did the shyness would never go away fully. I couldn't understand why I was cursed with this shyness, all it did was ruin opportunities I could have had to connect with new souls, as well improving my social life. "Why me?" "This wasn't something that you're born with, so why?" "What's the worst that could happen?" "All I have to do is talk." These are all thoughts I had at some point in my life and they all collectively clouded my mind. In turn, they bred an insecure black man for years on end. I really viewed myself as a defect. I felt there was something truly wrong with me. Not having the ability to communicate properly made me dislike myself intensely. Especially coming from a family of extroverted individuals, I genuinely believed there were mistakes made in the process of my creation. My insecurities, lack of confidence, and lack of awareness of what my purpose was all intensified my level of shyness. For years I was a shell of negativity. As I have gotten to know myself more, I became more comfortable with the idea of who I am, but it was a long, tumultuous road that I traveled to get to this state mentally. My feelings on my shyness today are not as harsh as they were. I have learned to accept that side of me. So looking back at how I was compared to how I am currently, I would say I have come a long way in terms of my ability to communicate in a non-sweaty state. Now I view my shyness as a manifestation of my subconscious trying to help me avoid toxic energies.

I am not sure if that is true at all, but I feel sometimes you must come up with reasons even if they are not true to bring yourself closer towards accepting who you are. If you repeat something long enough, it will become true, isn't that how manifestation works? For me, my mind creates realities that are the furthest thing from true but usually in a negative way. So I try to use that fact to my advantage and tell myself things that are for the betterment of my mental state, even if it's not true initially, it will become real eventually. Maybe not the healthiest step towards change but it works for me. If you are a shy individual, I suggest you move towards change at your own pace. There is no rush to try to change that part of you, I recommend you try at least once a week and force yourself into an uncomfortable state. Push yourself out of that shy side, and just talk to someone random with the intention of dismantling that shyness. The odds of it working out in your favor in your head may seem less but if the saying "thoughts become things" is true, if you dial your brain to a positive line of thinking, you'll be a non-shy individual in 30 days or less. Whether it be online or in person interactions, do what makes you feel comfortable enough to make your conversational skills improve. Forcing myself into constant uncomfortable interactions brought me so much closer towards acceptance of the shyness and further away from the days where I let it control me. I encourage anyone who deals with a bit of shyness to not view themselves as defective. Put a positive spin on your "flaws" and let that positive line of thinking move you even closer towards acceptance of them. None of my advice may hold weight at any point being that I am speaking from a dark space, but I see the light. I know change is possible, so my advice comes a hopeful place. I hope you can trust it. I am sure shyness has held me back from a lot of dope connections and opportunities but here I remain with less sweat under my arms as well as an even less of a shy attitude. It is still here regardless of the progress I have made but now I embrace it. I accept it and I know this is what makes me, ME. While there are shy individual's in the world, some probably reading this sentence, my level of shyness cannot be duplicated. I accept this version of my uniqueness no matter how detrimental it has been. You were born the way you are for a reason and what that reason is on you to decide fully but there were no mistakes in your inception. Shyness is a very normal trait to have that can either consume the entirety of who you are as a person or just be a small fragment of your being. If remaining shy and only interacting with those who make you comfortable is what you want, then you should stay with that. If you want to turn your desire to change and interact more into a reality, then you are going to have visit that uncomfortable, sweaty, nervous state regularly in order for true change to come. I dial back to shy sides even with the growth I have had on my journey but when I accepted this shyness as a part of me not have it against me, I became more comfortable within. Accept and progress or remain still and not change. The choice is yours, so live how you want but make sure you are at peace with what route you choose.

52-STABILITY

ACTUAL DEFINITION - THE STATE OF BEING STABLE

MY DEFINITION - AN ACHIEVABLE GOAL

Obtaining stability is the ultimate goal in my life. I want everything in my life to be completely stable and for that to happen, I need every goal I have in my mind to be manifested: I need my financial situation to be consistent enough for me to never miss a bill, with money left over to do what I want with, I need my family, friends, and partner to be safe and satisfied within every aspect of their lives; and I need all my creative endeavors to be widely accepted, appreciated, and remembered. The only way I can get all those things is to work as hard as I can until I have them, the most simple but difficult thing to do ever. Chasing stability is such an exhausting journey and the scariest part about it all is that so many different factors (many of them being random) can cause the journey to never end. Life is extremely unpredictable but even knowing that fact, it is not wise to acknowledge it consistently. So, what do we do? What I learned from my journey towards stability is to move forward, relentlessly with all your being and to maintain a positive thought process along the way. You may think this is hypocritical being that I expressed at many points during this book how much I overthink and how I let fear guide me through life. If you had that thought, I do not blame you. I DO overthink every step I take but the one thought I maintain while that is happening is that I WILL make it. It took me so long to figure out what I was actually good at in life and even longer to conjure up the confidence to attempt to turn what I am good at into something profitable. However, once both of those were checked off the list, the rest was easy to figure out. I would never be able to forgive myself if I quit before I was ahead, so I owe it to myself and to all the others in my life who have aided and supported me along the way to earn that stable life I am working towards. It is extremely ironic that the journey towards stability is very shaky, but it is possible to get that reality yourself if you so desire it. I know it is. I have seen too many individuals get a life they desired/manifested and although I am not following their blueprint as my own, their victories are something I pay attention to almost obsessively. The reason I pay attention to other people's journeys so closely is strictly for inspirational purposes. I try not to compare my life to anybody else's but its unavoidable at times during this process. I like to see reminders of what is possible for a hard worker consistently. If you work hard and stay focused, you can have the life you desire. So I pay attention to the winners for extra motivation; I am aware I am being hypocritical. How can you be focused and pay attention to other people's wins? To that I say, whoever I am watching and what I am doing are two different routes that are being traversed. Although I am inspired, I am not emulating. I am able to apply the inspiration gained to my own journey which in turn causes me to work ten times harder. Being on social media, reading articles, etc., you see all the time that people have made it and on paper, they live comfortably-but who knows, their lives could be way worse now that they have that stability. All I know is when I achieve my own version of a stable life, I know I will be able to handle the unstable moments better than I do now.

Maybe that's overconfidence or just a naive way of thinking but my belief in myself goes that deep and I know I can do it if I try. If stability within your life is what you truly desire, just know you will trip, fall, and cannot get up a few times as you walk down the path towards your destiny, but you have to keep going NO MATTER WHAT. Whether the blockades come from an external source or internally in your mind, know they will come. If you move with awareness of their existence and the ignorance of their impact on you, everything will work out in your favor. Gaining stability is not a stable process but beyond achievable.

53-SURPRISED

53-SURPISED

ACTUAL DEFINITION - FEELINGS OR SHOWING SURPRISE

MY DEFINITION – NOT

Nothing surprises me anymore. Everything that goes on the world does not shock me anymore. From the amount of hate that black people still receive till this day, to the amount it costs to have a roof over your head with a fully stocked fridge, I am not surprised at all at the craziness this world has to offer anymore. What I am truly not surprised about is people's ability to do me wrong no matter how transparent, honest, and real I am with them. This chapter may come off a bit whiny and if I am being honest, this is me venting fresh off a situation I just experienced. MY FEELINGS ARE HURT but again I am not surprised. As a black man whose community shies away from the men showing emotion, know this chapter will directly go against that stigma completely. Maybe I am a bad judge of character or I am too trusting, but I consistently have encountered human beings who have betrayed my trust/treated me unfairly and I am sick of it. I am self-aware enough to know that I am not perfect, my behavior may have been the trigger for them to shoot me in the back and I am also aware that I need to be more cautious and protective of my energy…but what can I say? They wear their disingenuous masks very well. I have been lied to, stolen from, abandoned during critical periods of my journey and it really does not get any easier no matter how many times it happens so what do I do? Embrace my introverted nature and limit my interactions? Keep the ones who have not folded yet and not let anyone else in? I am hurt but again I am not surprised that people can tap into a side of their heart that contradicts who they have presented themselves to be initially. I am not surprised. Betrayal, disloyalty, and hate have all persisted throughout the history. So why am I still affected by this knowing this fact? I should be self-aware enough and not be as sensitive to those facts, but as a human being, as a man who is in tune with his emotions, I cannot help but to feel hurt by these overly consistent situations I have been in with people I thought actually gave a fuck about me. I encourage everyone to express your frustrations and release especially if you have been through a similar stream of feelings like what I am expressing. If you have not been able to express yourself like me, if you keep it inside, you will implode and go crazy eventually. So I recommend you find a healthy outlet for your frustrations before it becomes too much to handle internally. I wish I could provide some sort of advice or wisdom on how to avoid the snakes in the grass but as I have clearly expressed, I am still learning the hard way and am reminded that they are hard to avoid. Move as cautiously as you can. As I am growing, I am learning to separate my personal feelings from how people treat me. At certain points in life I would blame myself for allowing myself to get in these situations, but I had to learn what was happening to me wasn't a reflection of me. The negative behavior I was receiving reflected the true darkness that exists within the human condition. I needed to experience this in order to learn how to avoid this type of energy. I cannot escape this dark energy, but I am learning to grow through the moments of frustration by talking about it or in this case, write a whole chapter of my book about how I feel and what I have been through.

Disingenuous individuals existed before the planet took shape and they will (unfortunately) continue to exist after all of this is said and done. Unfortunately, I will probably go through this again, but I hope this path of pain leads to the land of genuine individuals only. One can only hope but being that a world full of genuine people is a farfetched concept, all I can do is be smarter and more precise in the vetting process when bringing new individuals in my life. BE CAREFUL WHO YOU TRUST.

54-THINK

54-THINK

ACTUAL DEFINITION - HAVE A PARTIUCULAR OPINION, BELIEF OR IDEA ABOUT SOMEONE OR SOMETHING

MY DEFINITION - AN ABILITY THAT IS DONE TOO MUCH AND NOT ENOUGH SIMULTANEOUSLY

Full transparency on how this chapter came about and why I chose this word. I promise it is not that deep of an explanation: While sitting staring blankly at my computer screen for almost a half an hour, I was repeating the word "think" and it hit me like a bag of bricks to choose this word as the next chapter. Literal thinking bred this chapter which proves part of my definition of this word true, overthinking caused this.

My fellow over-thinkers can relate to how tough it is to make decisions, not overanalyze every conversation you have, not think about what you are doing three weeks from now. A very exhausting process to say the least. I have literally overthought my way out of potential blessings, and the only cure I have learned to utilize for my overthinking is breathing and centering myself into a state where my thoughts are aligned in an organized way. I am not sure if that even makes sense to you, but it works for me. If that does not work, I make sure to have someone in my life who really cares about me on standby and get them to yell at me enough till I am back to normal. Two unique, not guaranteed to work methods but those are what have worked for me at times. On the flip side of my life, sometimes I do not think things through enough and make bad decisions especially when it comes to my words. I am not sure if my introverted nature blessed with me the ability to burst out my passion easier, but I have a very difficult time filtering my thoughts, so I end up saying exactly what's on my mind regardless of anyone else's feelings. It is a problem that has gotten a lot of feelings hurt as well as both of sides of my face very sore due to a well-deserved slap. Although those things have happened more than once, I still stand by the fact that people need the truth in order to change their ways, and this is coming from the most sensitive black man you will probably ever encounter. So, although I plan to express my truth no matter how much backlash/pain I receive, going forward I will do it in a more controlled state. Keep a healthy balance of overthinking and not thinking at all and I believe most decisions that will be made are coming from a centered/controlled state. In addition, if what I just said was too poetic, I will say it in simpler terms. Think before you speak as often as you can. Say what you mean and mean what you say but think before you spit out a sentence because if you do not, you are bound to hurt some feelings like I have. Also, if someone is attempting to slap you in your face for expressing your truth, clearly you did not think long enough before speaking and you really should invest in martial arts classes so you can learn how to dodge just in case if this keeps happening. If there is anything I want you to take from this chapter, it is to understand I have lived through every negative outcome of a situation that either my mind created or manifested because of my behavior, so when I attempt to provide you with words of wisdom, it is so you can avoid ending up like me. You're welcome. I am the sacrificial lamb that will guide you towards a path of peace. Thinking before acting can cause an overthought outcome that will leave you in a paralyzing state. On the flip side, not thinking enough can cause nothing but a bad outcome no matter the situation. I have experienced both the positive and negative outcomes that comes from thinking and while I do it too much and not enough simultaneously, I know I will eventually think myself into a state of stillness. I know this constant thinking will conjure the reality I desire eventually. My mind will be quiet enough for me to actually control the words that come out of my mouth one of these days. Until then, I am saying what I want, when I want.

55-TIME

55-TIME

ACTUAL DEFINITION - THE INDEFINITE CONTINUED PROGRESS OF EXISTENCE AND EVENTS IN THE PAST, PRESENT AND FUTURE REGARDED AS A WHOLE

MY DEFINITION - INESCAPBLE, UNAVOIDABLE, ALWAYS FLOWING, NEVER ENDING, USE YOURS WISLEY

Time waits for no guy or gal. The clock never stops ticking. Before you are born, while you are alive, and after you die, time is the only constant. Scary huh? My thoughts have led me to think more as I have gotten older and I started to feel that time moves faster and faster each year. Whether that's due to the rapid number of experiences I am having or the amount of information the internet floods my brain with, I truly wish it would slow down sometimes. Time is a part of our lives whether we are using or wasting. Every moment has some significance and is so unique because it can never be recaptured again. So not only does time move so fast that everything flows whether we like it or not, but it also can never ever come back. Think back to when you were a child and analyze where you are currently in life and try to calculate exactly how much time down to the minute that has passed since you were in diapers. I am sure it is an insane amount of time that is lost forever and does not exist outside our own memories. My intense depression has eliminated a large amount of my memories I have experienced. Whether it is for my benefit or not, the large chunk of years where I was in the darkness, I do not remember. Who I was, what I was doing, and even why I was so depressed are gone forever. All that time is gone. Our time here can be taken away from us in an instant in many ways. Luckily, there are just as many ways to live life to the fullest before that happens. For time to be such an ethereal and endless constant, our ability to control it not as equally incredible.

I personally try not (but fail) to acknowledge the invisible expiration date we all have and honestly that awareness that I have of the fact that we aren't here forever motivates me to use every hour of each day that I have available to do what I have to do in order to solidify my chances of transcending in peace. I have a bit of fear that my time will end before my soul is satisfied but time will permit a reality of its choice without my say so I should not be as fearful knowing it's out of my hands. Right? Such a terrifying thought but I know my time here is impactful and necessary. The utilization of your time here on earth (or wherever you come from) is ultimately up to you. What and where you decide to distribute your time and energy is your decision but make it count and make it worthwhile. I feel through my procrastination and fear I wasted a lot of my time here. Although I maintain some regrets, that fact motivates me to use what time I have left to do everything I want. As I have started to align closer with my purpose, I feel I am on my second wind. The years spent being depressed and nonproductive I do not remember that well but every day I have spent doing what I love I will never forget. I feel revitalized and more focused than ever on everything but time.

So, what is the best way to utilize our time here on earth? The most direct and cliché answer I can give is, do what you love. Do what makes your soul sing. Do what makes your twinkie tingle with no regrets or hesitation because time will continue to go on without you. So if you do not catch up, you will miss out. The days, months, years, and eons will go by and your time will eventually be up (until you are reincarnated as a bird or something). So you utilize those same amount days, months, and years, doing what brings you peace.

56-TIMING

ACTUAL DEFINITION - THE CHOICE, JUDGEMENT, OR CONTROL OF WHEN SOMETHING SHOULD BE DONE

MY DEFINITION - A FRUSTRATING CONCEPT TO AN IMPATIENT AND PASSIONATE CREATIVE

I hate waiting. I have zero patience. I want what I want/deserve when I want it. A childish mindset but that is just how I am, I never claimed to be an adult, society just placed this title on me when I turned a certain age. I tie my impatience with my birth. I was born many months earlier than expected and I always looked at that fact as me saying "fuck this, I can't wait anymore, it is time to see the world" and hopped out the womb in October as opposed to some other boring month. A ridiculous thought but I truly believe I was born with an impatient attitude. So when you try to mention TIMING to me, I immediately get frustrated at the thought of waiting for what I want/deserve. I am fully aware this type of attitude is beyond childish and unrealistic, but I simply do not care. If I put in a consistent amount of hours at work daily, weekly, monthly, and yearly and still don't have what I want/deserve while I'm being told "timing is everything" "just be patient: WHY WOULDN'T I GET UPSET?!

On the flip side of everything I am saying, I am fully aware this attitude is a detriment to my progression. Being comfortable with the fact that things will happen on a time that is not in my control is the hardest realization to swallow. I am sure all my fellow ambitious entrepreneurs can semi relate to this feeling. Having razor sharp focus on specific goals can come easily while simultaneously distracting you. Ultimately having you miss moments along the way while traveling towards your goals. My focus has been centered on my ultimate goal in life which is to heal the world with my art/energy and help as many people as I can along the way. I will admit I have not made time to slow down and start appreciating the journey leading up to those goals but disconnecting from the end goal is so hard. When you have done nothing but travel aimlessly through life depressed without a real sense of what your purpose is to then end up discovering it, paired with the willingness to grasp it, it is hard to slow down and understand the concept of "timing". The fear of missing out on the one chance to have what you want is something I try not to acknowledge because it is nothing more than anxiety, the fear of what could happen, but it is hard to stop. It is hard to shift your focus to move from anything but forward. Having the blinders up and having an intense focus on your goals is actually even more blinding when compared to "smelling the roses". Maintaining the balance between remaining focused and enjoying the journey is very difficult for me. The razor sharped focus breeds exhaustion, so I try to be cognizant of my energy levels and rest while I can, when I can. I feel if I sit for too long, I will lose my momentum and not work as hard and on the flip side I feel if I go too hard, I will burn myself out into a state where I do not have the energy to enjoy the fruits of my labor. As a Libra, you would expect me to have some form of familiarity of balance but again, the struggle between my mind, body, and spirit need to be aligned before I can apply the concept of balance to my life, rather than simply understanding it. Unfortunately, the process of trying to mend the relationship between my mind, body, and spirit is happening in the middle of my entrepreneurial journey, so the process is taking a bit longer to be solved. I strive to find a balance between maintaining a solid work ethic while simultaneously enjoying the moments and appreciating the concept of timing.

The endless battle I am trapped in is the side of life where the outcomes are either, I adapt the concept of timing to my life when it comes to my goals and the other side is where I maintain tunnel vision and work my ass off while not accepting anything less than what I want/deserve. Patience and Impatience. The never-ending battle in my mind. Both sides have positive and negative attributes to them and truthfully, it is an exhausting struggle to maintain. So from here on out, I vow to take the middle road and maintain a healthy balance of work ethic with razor sharped focus sprinkled in with a little impatience, mixed with a bit of patience and comfort with the thought that things are happening when they are supposed to. I will try but no guarantees. Every goal that I am working towards is waiting patiently for me, but I cannot patiently walk towards them. I recognize the journey is the most beautiful part of progression, but I want it all within my grasp on my time. I want what I deserve and deserve what I want but if the only way forward is at a pace that is out of my control, I GUESS I will just roll with the punches and (not happily) accept the conditions the universe has set for me. Timing happens on its own time and that's just a reality we all have to accept at some point.

57-TRANSPARENCY

57-TRANSPARENCY

ACTUAL DEFINITION - THE CONDITION OF BEING TRANSPARENT

MY DEFINITION - SOMETHING I NEED TO WORK ON

I am always not fully transparent with my feelings. My defense mechanism that kicks in when I am at the crossroads of being honest with someone about my feelings versus being aloof, both good and bad things usually end up occurring ending with me, either lying about how I feel and saying the opposite of how I actually feel, or I end up staying quiet. Sometimes I also try to change the subject as smoothly as I can. I believe I do this to protect myself from the judgement that I anxiously think I will receive from the other person involved so to avoid that I appeal to them in a way where what I say is what they want to hear with the only goal being to keep them in my life a bit longer. A very disingenuous and hypocritical approach that I try not take often but it comes out subconsciously and if it was not for my intense self-reflection, I may not have noticed this bad habit. What I am doing is not being honest and not truly valuing the relationship I have with this person and I know it is a terrible thing to do (trust me I am working on it) but I have a very hard time losing people I care about. You're probably thinking "if you're just honest all the time the ones in your life will respect you more and be more inclined to stay in your life as opposed to you lying and pushing them further away" YES, I agree with you if these are your thoughts, but it is literally out of fear that this defense mechanism activates. I have been abandoned, betrayed, and let down by many people I care about in certain moments from me simply expressing my honest feelings/for other reasons and those experiences have left a deep gash on my soul that will not be easily repaired. I am aware I have to get out of that fear in order to preserve my relationships, I am aware that I HAVE to be honest with my feelings in order to heal from all the bullshit I have been through, but it is very hard. The level of trauma I have experienced is not easy to sweep under the rug and I am also aware it could come off like I am making excuses for my behavior (there are none) but this is my truth, and I MUST acknowledge these things in order to move past them. I dislike being judged, I dislike being abandoned, I dislike hurting people, I dislike not being transparent and in order for me to change those feelings to all positives I have to change my behavior. If you are reading this and can relate to this in any way I encourage you to do what I am doing in this chapter: to acknowledge your behavior (does not have to be in book form) and actively try to correct it before you end up with a deep scar on your soul like mine. My awareness of my behavior and my motivation to change are not synonymous. A shift needs to occur sooner than later. For the ones who are reading this who empathize with my feelings and feel any kind of sadness for me I am not deserving of those feelings at all and you should save them for someone who is worthy of them. I do not feel like a good person for lying and not being transparent with the ones who I claim to care about so much. I am damaged goods who must repair himself internally in order to keep what I value externally. To those who disagree with my approach and have been frustrated with my behavior throughout this chapter your feelings are warranted, and I deserve any and all criticism thrown my way. I am learning to accept my imperfectness and I strive to be a better me. I want to be a better me. I must do better and be better. Ridding yourself of your toxic traits/bad habits is a process that is equally as long as healing from trauma, progressing entrepreneurial etc. As I have said multiple times throughout this book, the one thing that I keep repeating as a reminder to myself (and you) is your desire for change must be equal to the amount of work you put in towards obtaining the change you seek. Desire with no work is counterproductive and no true change will manifest. This chapter is probably the most transparent I have been about myself, with myself so I hope my efforts aren't for nothing. I will follow through with my desire to change once the experience of facing myself is over. Lastly,

I ask that you keep me your heart, prayers, and mind going forward. By the time, the next book around my transparency will be front and center and I will be a changed author. I promise.

58-WANT

58-WANT

ACTUAL DEFINITION - HAVE A DESIRE TO POSSESS OR DO (SOMETHING), WISH FOR

MY DEFINITION - AN INESCAPABLE FEELING/DESIRE.

Thinking back on my life as an only child, the majority of things I wanted in life whether it be games or clothes I always got it in one way or another. Whether it be as a gift from a family member or through my own means, I always got what I want. It was not always exactly when I wanted it, but it still ended up in my possession somehow and I feel that is where my ability to balance my "wants" and :"needs" really started to waver. The impatience always eventually settled in and the annoyance of not having what I wanted sparked like a match and ultimately grew into a flame of frustration that clouded my judgement which caused one of two outcomes. It either made me act in a childish way or caused me to spend whatever I had in that moment to get what I wanted when I wanted it. Not responsible. Not smart. A common occurrence in my life (even till this day at times) that I eventually will eliminate. Having the desire to want things for yourself is okay but there must be level of realism mixed in those thoughts (this advice is for you but mostly for me) and you need to realize those "wants" may not be the best thing for you in those moments where you are really wanting whatever it is. We all want something out of this life (I hope) something we damn near crave, so bad that the inescapable desire of wanting that one thing drives us mad. While on my journey throughout my life one thing I have learned is that patience and acceptance play a huge role in the pace we keep when working towards making those "wants" be ours. Wants and expectations go hand and hand especially if you have some familiarity with getting what you want, so patience is crucial during that time. While you wait till you get that thing you desire the acceptance of the fact that you may not get it at all becomes easier to deal with the longer the wait is between the wanting and obtaining phases. As I am writing this, I am simultaneously reflecting on my past experiences dealing with my wants, I am realizing maturity plays a major role as well. The tolerance for not getting what you want when you are younger (in my case) is much shorter and as you grow your familiarity with the harsher sides of reality become easier to deal with (most of the time). I am thinking back to times in my life where I wanted something specific online, but I was in between checks that week and while I had the money in my account to get what I wanted, it was not smart to touch that money, so what did I do? You guessed it. I could not resist the urge of my wants and compulsively spent that money that I ended needing a few days later for an unexpected broken tire.

Smart right?

There have been times in my life where I have wanted certain things so bad when I finally got it, all the excitement I had for its arrival was eliminated completely as soon as I looked down into my lap and laid my eyes on it. Till this day I do not know why this has happened but the fact that this has happened repeatedly helped realign my focus on what is important and what isn't. The feeling of wanting something is nothing more than a feeling. Our minds convinces us once we get what we desire it will equate to a feeling just as stimulating as the one prior to reaching the checkout screen but that's not the case at all. Recognizing the feeling of "want" and reward is something I wish I adapted to sooner than later. In addition, my wants have consumed me so deeply that they have caused me to spend money that was meant for bills and then I am left broke. All I am left with the feeling of a different kind of "want" and an empty bank account. The never-ending cycle of wanting never ends, especially if you are an ambitious, slightly greedy individual like myself. Maturity, awareness, patience, acceptance are all important factors when considering going for something you want in life. Whether it be a goal or a few items in your Amazon cart, do not be in a rush to get it. Indulge in the feeling of "want" when it makes complete sense in your mind and makes even more sense financially. It is possible to obtain anything you want, just expect a long waiting process/paired with a lot minutes, hours, days, months, and years putting the work in to get it in a time that aligns with timeline you have in your head. If you are not the type to wait hopefully you won't end up dissatisfied and broke like I have been at times. Be mindful of every action you take when heading towards your wants. Do not get caught in the cycle of wanting, most times it won't end in your favor positively. PATIENCE. What you want is not going anywhere, the opportunity to get it when you desire may dissipate depending on your patience level. Do not forget. PATIENCE.

59-WRITE

ACTUAL DEFINITION - MARK (LETTERS, WORDS, OR OTHER SYMBOLS) ON A SURFACE, TYPICALLY PAPER,WITH A PEN,PENCIL,OR SIMILAR IMPLEMENT

MY DEFINITION - AN ESCAPE, A TALENT. AN ART. MY FIRST LOVE.

I love writing. I love the freedom that comes with writing. I love the vulnerability I can have when I am writing. I love the level of honesty I can achieve through writing. I love the possibilities and change that can happen internally/externally that come from writing. I love the possibilities of being able to become an inspiration for others that can come from writing. I have loved writing this book. This has been the most therapeutic and eye-opening experience I think I will ever have in my entire life. Most of what has been written was my first time acknowledging/expressing and I think I chose the healthiest medium to face myself. I first fell in love with writing at some point during grade school, I am not sure exactly what age I was around this time, but I know it was middle school. I remember English was always my favorite subject. I think it was my favorite mostly because the skills I learned in those classes were an actual benefit to my life while the other classes were just filler in my opinion, but I digress, English was the fucking best. I vividly remember one of my English teachers by the name of Mr. Capron (not sure if I spelled his name right-my apologies if you are reading this) who was the absolute best. I didn't know much about him outside of his job as my teacher, but he was a super tall white dude who always had the biggest smile and for some reason every time I saw him I envisioned him as a solider prior to teaching. No idea why but he was built like a super soldier compared to my middle schooler frame Some of his mannerisms and even the way he spoke led me to think he had some sort of southern solider like background. Even the way he would discipline us would was very authoritarian like, but his version was much gentler than that of general ordering his soldiers. I wish I got confirmation if any of this is actually true but the way my kid brain worked at the time is what caused this line of thinking.

Anyways, his patience, soothing personality, and voice, as well as his genuine love for the art of writing made each class and assignment worth indulging in rather than looking out the window waiting till the day ended. My memory may be a bit off which would not be surprising, but I think I got introduced to my favorite type of writing assignment in his class. It was the type of assignment where all you were given was just a picture and it was the students job to create a story based off what we see. The absolute best and a true test of creativity. This type of assignment was the best for me because I was heavily locked into my introverted side very early on and all I did was think and create scenarios/stories in my brain all day long so every assignment like this was effortless to me. In my other classes that I was not as interested in I created stories in my head to get me through the day, so I knew I would get an A on every assignment like this.

You really get to flex your brain and use your imagination during these assignments and as a kid I feel that is super important because it allows you to tap into the side of your brain that will serve you better than the sugary candies and television we all indulged in around then as kids. Every single one of those type of assignments I passed with flying colors and Mr. Capron would always reassure me that I was a talented writer, he would try to tell me how proud he was of me and how good my writing was. During those moments when that happened, I was so awkward at the time I probably just smiled, nodded, and walked away but deep down those words of affirmation were everything to me and gave me the confidence I needed to pursue this passion of mine and I am eternally grateful to Mr. Capron as well as all the other English teachers I had. Words of affirmation cut differently as a kid, and if your upbringing was like mine where you didn't get too many too often getting them in a place you don't really enjoy being made the experience of school slightly more enjoyable.

Parents encourage your children to write/indulge fully into whatever their interest may be. Allow them the freedom to choose what that is but when they find it early on and you notice some skill, that they have at it make sure they indulge in it as much as they can. Encourage and motivate them to keep going. When I have children of my own, I will do for them what was not done for me. Educators provide your students with reassurance and genuine support. Give them words of affirmation as often as you can Former students go back into your brain and try to remember a teacher that made an impact on your life in a positive way. I am sure you can find at least one, they deserve your appreciation. Teachers it means the world to us when you encourage us especially during those crucial developmental stages of our lives. If you're a fellow writer know you're in control of your work from start to finish. Write about anything. Write about nothing. Just write continuously and I promise your soul will sing and you will free yourself from a lot of negative thoughts/energy.

I love the art/experience of writing so much and yet I typed all of this. I am a fraud huh?

60-END

60-END

ACTUAL DEFINITION - A FINAL PART OF SOMETHING, ESPECIALLY A PERIOD OF TIME, AN ACTIVITY, OR A STORY

THE FURTHEST OR MOST EXTREME PART OR POINT OF SOMETHING

MY DEFINITION - ALL GOOD THINGS COME TO AN END BUT IN MY CASE THE NEGATIVE THINKING AND WORDS I HAVE USED TO DESCRIBE MYSELF WILL END

The journey leading up this final chapter of the book has been beyond exhausting, filled with many pauses during my writing process due to my lack of motivation, intense depression, and me not allotting specific blocks of time in my week to write but here we are, the end. This book has been beyond reflective and the majority of things that were written in previous chapters were thoughts that I fully acknowledged for the first time while writing it out and most of what was written were things I suppressed for years. I was not strong enough to experience the feelings that came with those thoughts until

I started this book. I learned during this process that I did not take accountability for much of behavior, thoughts, and position in life until I decided to deeply self-reflect and travel the avenue within me. A lot of what I complained about, a lot of what made me depressed, a lot of changes I desired but never worked towards, are all because of me. I have been in my own way for the entirety of my life. My lack of awareness of who I am caused so much pain to good women who entered my life. Without this experience, I am sure I would still be stuck on that toxic, unaware path. No longer will I remain this way. This book is also a proof of concept. Proof that any idea can turn into something tangible and life changing if you stay consistent/forward thinking for long enough. This book allowed me to prove to myself that if you stick with something long enough you can create something magical if you endure the challenging roadblocks that your mind creates. Before writing the first page I had so much doubt that I would not be able to stick with this for so long, especially after I lost all my work that already took so much out of me, I was just counting the days till I gave up. I proved myself wrong and I could not be prouder. This book is the first tangible piece of work that I stuck with and manifested. This book is my healing process in tangible form. No matter all the roadblocks that I let get/put in my way, this is the first thing I have done in my life that I am truly proud of accomplishing and probably the first time I am genuinely proud of myself. I have healed so much during the process of creating The Avenue, I feel so much lighter and although this book is done my journey towards a fully healed state is far from being over. I strive to continue down the path towards being totally acceptive of who I am and what position in the universe I am placed in. The creation of this book has started me on a path towards a life where I stop thinking and talking negatively about myself. This book has led me down a path where I will strive to cultivate stronger relationships with family, friends, and myself. This book has made more aware of who I am and how I act. I am sure at times when I repeated something negative about myself you rolled your eyes or got frustrated with me and if so, I apologize. If you got upset, if I triggered or annoyed you at any point, I am sorry. That was not my intention, but I had to be as transparent as possible to find out what was going on with me. I will not apologize for being myself, however. To tell my story I had to be my authentic self and although certain portions of this tale were written at different times in my life every moment centers back to who I am at my core. An overthinking, ambitious, introverted, individual. My transparency is meant to inspire you to work towards living in your own truth and begin your own path of healing. Through self-reflection and intense soul searching I found out more about myself, than I ever expected too. This experience is all I want for you especially if you feel just as lost as I was. I am not a motivational speaker, I am not a therapist, I am not an expert, I am not even a seasoned author (forgive me for any typos) but I am a human being who is becoming more aware of his emotions, traumas, and understanding of why and how he is the way he is. I am someone who gladly will be the poster boy for imperfection. I will gladly be the example of an individual who is not the ideal person with the healthiest mental state who's trying to change if it means I can inspire others to own who they are and do the same. The process of creating this book broke and built me in so many ways, and I believe everything from the beginning of this book to this very sentence is reflective of who I am, who I was, and who I am striving to be.

Thank you for embarking on the journey of the destruction and construction of who I WAS and who I am GOING to be. Find your avenue and walk down it no matter how turbulent the journey is. Walk within to change your reality. There is a path for all of us and it is really ultimately up to you if you decide to take that road. Endure and survive the stresses life throws your way and you will end up ascending way further than you ever could have imagined. Move forward with the awareness that the road within will uncover truths that at times will be painful, move with the awareness that you will need to break yourself down into pieces in order be reconstructed into an impenetrable version of yourself. Find your avenue and walk with your head held high. You can change too.

61-THANK YOU

THANK YOU

If you have made it this far, to the very end of my first book I want to say THANK YOU. I am not entirely sure whose hands this book has ended up in, but I am eternally grateful you decided to indulge and make it to the very end. My apologies to the hardcore book fanatics, professional authors, and anyone else who noticed any spelling errors, grammatical errors, or if my writing style is at the level of an amateur. If my story annoyed, you at any point I am grateful you managed to deal with it till the very end. Maybe this is just my insecure overthinking nature kicking in, but I am aware I am not an expert in this, but everything you just read was an extension of my spirit without any filter. My only intention when coming into this book was to put my emotions, feelings, and experiences at the forefront without any reservations, with the goal to find healing/acceptance with who I am. I believe I did this in the most authentic way I could. The journey with this book was almost a four-year long process, but here I am writing one of the very last pages of this book, so crazy but I hope by me saying that and having this book be in your hands- is the purest example of what my perseverance and consistency helped create. All I hope is that this book has inspired you in any way. I hope it made you find the strength to take a look inside yourself and find the confidence to find the change you desire. I wanted you to acknowledge your imperfections as well as your strengths. This book means the world to me and I hope that if it means anything to you, you will pass it along to as many people as you think may need what you gained from reading this. Again (for like the 5th time), I thank you from the bottom of my heart for indulging in my first piece of tangible art and I hope you enjoyed your brief stay within my mind. See you next time!

This book is dedicated to everyone who wears their imperfections and truth on their sleeve. As you may have noticed (probably from the first chapter), I have so much to work on internally. I am in a space in life where I am trying to ascend to the next level in my life, but I am simultaneously holding myself back, and part of the purpose for creating this book was to face these negative parts of my mind head on and ultimately find some sort of healing afterwards. This was an extremely healthy process, honestly even healthier for me than the therapy sessions I paid for during the course of writing this. I am PROUD of what I have done with this book, and regardless of the sales, reception, and accolades this book receives (it will receive a lot of each god willing) this book was written to heal me first and inspire the reader second. I wanted you to look me at me as the clearest example of what not to be, to not adapt my negative way of thinking and heal in a less turbulent way. I do believe the first and last step towards healing is garnering the confidence to face your issues head on and consistently hold yourself accountable at all times. If you must go as far as writing a book about yourself to speed up your healing process. This book took me four long years to complete, and I went through so many challenges (mostly internally) to get this done. I hope you enjoyed your brief stay on The Avenue, and I hope you will come back in the future and indulge in the next few books I will release. Hopefully, next time around I will not be in my own way as much and it will not be such a long-drawn-out process to release. No matter what you go through in life remember to move forward, relentlessly.

- JEFFREY A. KELLY

Twitter-@ThtAmbitiousguy Instagram-

@TheAve360

Made in the USA
Columbia, SC
22 May 2021

38381751R00161